JOURNEY TOWARDS PROFESSIONALISM:

STRAIGHT
TALK
FOR
TODAY'S
GENERATION

JOURNEY TOWARDS PROFESSIONALISM:

STRAIGHT
TALK
FOR
TODAY'S
GENERATION

A No-Nonsense Lesson about the Basics of Being a
Professional Aimed at Today's Generation.

JONATHAN R. KEY

iUniverse, Inc.
Bloomington

JOURNEY TOWARDS PROFESSIONALISM:
STRAIGHT TALK FOR TODAY'S GENERATION
**A No-Nonsense Lesson about the Basics of Being a
Professional Aimed at Today's Generation.**

iUniverse books may be ordered through booksellers or by contacting:

iUniverse
1663 Liberty Drive
Bloomington, IN 47403
www.iuniverse.com
1-800-Authors (1-800-288-4677)

ISBN: 978-1-4697-3237-4 (sc)
ISBN: 978-1-4697-3238-1 (ebk)

Printed in the United States of America

iUniverse rev. date: 12/30/2011

To all those who continually disregard me,
underestimate my potential or write me off.
Because you tell me what I can't do,
who I shouldn't be,
or what I'll never accomplish,
you inadvertently set the level of expectation
by which I must exceed my goals.

I humbly thank you.

Table of Contents

INTRODUCTION

THIS BOOK IS FOR THOSE who would like to be more professional in the workplace. This book is also for those younger generations just starting out in the workplace. Being a professional in the workplace is not limited to those who work in an office. You can find professionals in every form of business. Professionals work in retail, fast food, full service restaurants, temp services, schools, office buildings or the medical community. Being professional does not mean you have to wear a suit and tie. You can be a professional and wear a uniform. Professionalism is an attitude that starts with the desire to achieve more.

The problem is the same everywhere. Fewer and fewer employees in the workplace today have the knowledge of what it takes to be a professional. The majority desires more for themselves professionally and they do try to achieve it. However most never get to the next level because they don't know what it takes to actually get there. This trend is especially evident with those just out of high school all the way up to those in their mid-thirties and sometimes further. It is my desire to do something about that trend.

My name is Jonathan Key. Technically I am the Author, but I don't consider myself some famed and creative literary genius. I am just the guy who wrote this book. First

I want share with you some background. This insight will help set a few things in place on the playing field that is this book.

I did not start out any better than you. I am not special. I am not rich nor do I have any silver spoons given to me from my family. I was never popular in school nor have I been since. I have had more than my fair share of tough situations and bad breaks. I am not pretty, I am not beautiful and I am not skinny. By most counts, my personal background is exceedingly *average*.

However, this book is about professionalism. A person who has achieved any level of success in the business world usually has a long, professional history. Most individuals who are considered professionals have paid their dues to get where they are today. I have known a lot of professionals that made it to the top. But few actually share that history, or at least they don't share the parts you could learn something from.

I have that professional history. I have that professional experience, lots of it. That is what I am sharing with you in this book.

I have been in the workforce since my early teens. I started at the bottom, the very bottom. In order to move up I took advantage of every opportunity that came my way. Sometimes I went out and found that opportunity. I have been fired and quit and have done both in the crummy jobs and great jobs. I have worked for many different companies in various professional fields. I have worked in the blue collar, grease under your fingernails world. I have also sat next to CEO's of companies with a billion dollars in revenue and called them by their first name. I have written policies, procedures and regulations for many different companies and been the one to enforce them. At the professional management level I have more than a decade of time served under my belt.

Hard time served too I might add.

I have interviewed and hired hundreds of people in my professional experience and I have fired half as many. I have been in the position of being the sole person responsible for what gets done and I have had staff numbering in the hundreds. I have been in small businesses and I have managed businesses with tens of millions of dollars of revenue per year. I have been at the top, and the bottom, and I have made the trip more than once.

I had to learn as I went and most of the time and I learned the hard way. Sometimes the lessons I learned in the business world came at great personal and professional expense. I have been around enough to have seen it all in the business world. That's a fact.

That fact is evident to me more and more because I see people in the workforce today making the same mistakes I made, the *same* ones! Then one day I thought "If they only knew . . ."

Ding! All of the sudden in my head this book was born.

Imagine what you could do with some of those hard learned lessons. How much better off could you be if you didn't have to learn 1 or 2 things the hard way? What if there were a few things that you could just do differently which would put you ahead of the rest of the people like you out there? Would you listen? Would you take the advice of the battle scarred business veteran and avoid suffering those wounds yourself? Would it be worth it, is there value in those hard learned lessons?

I think so and I bet you do as well. That is why I wrote this book and that is why I hope you continue reading. I want to share with you the value of the lessons I learned the hard way so you can avoid the mistakes. I want you to know the basics of what you should be doing so that you can get ahead professionally. I can say to you with all honesty I want you to read this book and increase your chances of being able to succeed. You get all the benefit, all the gain.

Essentially in the business world you get to cut in line. You gain experience and knowledge without putting in any of the time and suffering the losses. That value, which will come from this book, is truly priceless. That value is yours for the taking and I hope you take advantage.

This book contains information that is short, sweet, blunt and to the point. There are 3 sections; *Getting in the Door*, *On the Job*, and *Moving Up*. The chapters in those sections will walk you through some of the traits of being professional from beginning to end. The chapters in each section are short enough that you won't have to kill yourself getting through it. And to reward you at the end of each chapter you get quickies! No not that; quickies are the pointed highlights of what you just read in that chapter! The notes are made for you so you don't have to worry about making them yourself. You should take the quickies and make them a daily part of your professional life. Send yourself emails and text messages with the quickie information in them. Put them on sticky notes in places you will see them. That way you can better utilize the pointers on a daily basis to light your way through your battles of being a professional!

I applaud you for putting forth the effort to read this book. By doing so you are already on your way to becoming a professional!

PART 1

GETTING
IN THE DOOR

THIS FIRST SECTION IS ABOUT getting you in the door at your chosen workplace. The information you read will lead you through many things that may or may not take place up until the point you start your first day of work. I am not trying to give you some comprehensive know-it-all guide; I am trying to keep you from stumbling around in the dark running into walls. You need to keep pointed in the right direction and moving forward during the entire process of getting on board with a new employer. The good news is you are going to get guidelines on how to do all of that! Of course those guidelines exclude finding the jobs to apply for. You are on your own for that.

Some of you may already have a job and may think, "Sweet, I get to skip the first section, I'm a third there because I already have a job!"

Please, *please* don't do that!

Did you ever take one of those trick tests in school? You know the one where the teacher says,

"Okay class, no talking during any part of this test. I am going to hand out the test over the subject we just studied, read the instructions, follow them, and turn it in when you are done. Good luck."

So you race through the test at top speed being as the test is only one page and 10 questions. They are easy questions too! You notice despite completing the test at record speed that you are one of the last of the class to turn in the test, but you are unsure as to why.

Then afterwards you fail the test! The teacher points out afterwards that the instructions, had you bothered to read them, said: 'Don't answer any questions, put your name on the top and turn in the test.'

(Insert the Homer Simpson "DOH!" here.)

Because you skipped the instructions you missed the point—and failed the test I might add. Well, that is my point. Don't skip anything, especially the beginning of this book! You may have a job already, but you will cover some topics that are not in the rest of the book. There is stuff you need to know, stuff you may not know, and stuff you might even know already. In any case, read it all just to be safe.

After reading the first section, you may gain some insight as to why you are stuck in the position you are in at the company you now work for. That is because being professional starts from the very beginning. If you are already in the workplace, read through the first section to see if you might have missed something. Take to heart the stuff that is new to you, make special note of it. Anything you already know can be a refresher. In the end it will all be worth remembering.

Chapter 1

The Challenges Ahead

YOUR JOURNEY HAS BEGUN! YOU want more from yourself professionally and damn it you should expect more! Wanting to better your current situation for yourself and possibly your family is a true sign of maturity. You already know that nobody is going to give anything to you; somehow I'll bet you figured that out the hard way. That tough lesson learned has put you on a journey to something better. That something better means being a professional at what it is you do.

The determination you possess will start to show to those around you. Your family will be impressed! They will start to see you becoming something great and should be happy, supportive and proud of you. Surrounding yourself with people that are supportive of your professional efforts will help you develop further. If they are not, blow 'em off. They probably haven't been there to support you in the past anyway, so you should be used to the disappointment by now.

The people that you consider friends will go in all different directions. Being a professional will start to show on the outside, and on you will feel it on the inside. Someday soon you will do something crazy like go home at a decent hour to get up for work the next day while your friends stay out and close down the bars. They will notice things like that and you will get a mixed response. Some will show understanding and some will not. Some may see the positive changes you are making and start to make their own changes in their lives. You could be an inspiration to some of your friends or you may alienate some of them. In either case let the chips fall where they may.

One of the things that will challenge your motivation of being professional will be the haters. Take special note of them, remember who they are. Use that haterisim to fuel your fire for success. What comes around goes around, and they will get theirs—I promise. They will give you grief about working for "the man", telling you that you sold out. They will be on you because you never hang out and party anymore. They will probably stop calling and being your friend all together (that is until they need something from you). They will write you off because your dedication to being professional looks like, to them, that you are acting like you are better than they are.

Guess what? You are.

Some of you were raised better than to think you are better than someone else. Allow me to elaborate. What matters when it comes to the pressures of dealing with all the haters is to remember where you are going. When you make the choices to be professional, you are doing so with a purpose. That purpose is something that only you understand and the haters do not. That purpose is so that one day you are better off than you are now. Tending bar, sacking groceries, or making $2.13 an hour may be where you are now; and we all have started there. What matters is where you are going. If you have an exact destination in mind, like a vice president spot, then good for you! Most of you do not have an end destination in mind. Keep pressing upwards no matter what and you will be surprised where you end up! Be going somewhere in your career and have a purpose. That makes you better off than half of the working force in America and better than most of your aimless friends. That is kind of sad and may hurt a little, but it is the truth. So when it comes to the haters, press on!

Another way to keep your professional fire going is to enjoy what you do. If you hate gaming and you work for a software game company you will have a hard time keeping a professional attitude. Career advisors say to do what you love. Of course most of us with our strange hobbies are not able to do what we love. You can, however, do something you like and really enjoy. One of the best ways for you to figure this out is to see a career counselor. There are many tests now days a career counselor can give you which will dig into what you like and don't like as a person. The results of those tests will point you in a direction of which career paths you might choose. These tests are very insightful and could show you careers you might not have otherwise thought of. By finding the link between things you enjoy and your job choice, you can make a more informed decision on a profession you can stay with for a long time. The happier you are, the more of a professional attitude you can maintain!

One of the biggest challenges I have come across with being professional is burn out. Those of you in your youth will be raring to go in your new career! Chances are that you will hit the ground on both feet and take off running at full speed towards your business goals. That is a great attitude to have! However, you end up working longer and harder for less. Then before you know it, what you used to love about your job you now hate. You stay tired and somewhat irritable which echoes in your professional attitude. To avoid that, take the time off you deserve when it is there. By all means go above and beyond in your career but don't kill yourself doing it. Having personally experienced this in my career already, I can attest that there are many more out there like me. Those who used to do something they loved and were good at, but then burned the candle at both ends of their job and soured themselves. The pursuit of money, status or recognition will speed up burnout. That is why you should enjoy your job as a professional while you are at work, and then leave your job at work when you get off. If you can maintain that balance it will help you avoid burn out and keep your professional desire at a high standard.

Be hard on yourself. The more you push yourself to do better the better you will become. You will have to sacrifice and it will make you angry sometimes. You will feel like you are excluding yourself from all the fun or others are leaving you out on purpose. Those feelings are okay! Do not dwell on the negative feelings, but look to all of the positives you are creating for yourself. Keep steady on the course you are laying out for yourself and remember; you are on your way to being professional! Don't make excuses; make your professional career happen. The only thing standing in your way is you.

CHAPTER 1 QUICKIES:

- Surround yourself with people that will support your choice to be professional.
- Do something you enjoy and can live with if you can't do what you love.
- Leave your work in the workplace to avoid burn out. Try not to take your work home.

Chapter 2

Looking in Your Closet

We have gone over what to expect in going down the road of being a professional in the last chapter. Now we will take that first step towards achieving that goal!

To give you a high level view of what to expect here what we will be going over is you. Your objective is to find out everything there is floating around out there about you. In a nutshell, you get to be your own stalker.

Good times, huh?

Every human resource manager worth their salt is reviewing you online. No matter how great your resume or how well you just interviewed, they go back to their desk and they all go to the same place.

Google. Then they start digging.

Even if you agree to let the company do a background or credit check upon the start of the hiring process (yes some do that!), they will look beyond those reports. They want to know what is floating around out there in cyberspace that is not on your resume. Someone could interview you and think you are top notch. Then, following a quick look on Google, see quite a few negative things and have a much different opinion. Heck you may be shocked and surprised as to what is out there, have you looked?

The first place you need to start is your Facebook or MySpace page. We will discuss the affects of your social media habits in a later chapter. For now, you just need to worry about cleaning up the place. Some of you may have some pretty unimpressive stuff on your social network pages when it comes to your employers' point of view. You will have to change your mind set when deciding to clean things up. Don't think like you normally would because you obviously don't see anything wrong with what you are doing now. Look at your pages though the eyes of a million dollar business owner who is a Sunday school teacher. Change your point of view to that and let it soak in for a while. Then go to your pages and have a look around.

You might be somewhat offended at what you see. If you can say with all honesty that your social pages are of the utmost moral standards, then you are better off than most. The rest of you will have your work cut out for you.

In short, what you are wanting to portray is a good wholesome image. Interaction and postings involving family and friends is perfectly acceptable. Beer bongs, keg stands and bachelor night at the strip club are not.

Be sure to look at all of your social networking sites, not just the Facebook or MySpace. Google and Yahoo along with dozens of other companies have started to take hold of the social media scene. Be sure and go through every site that you are a member of.

After that you should Google yourself and see what is out there. Look on Yahoo and MSN search engines as well. Be sure and go through several pages to make sure there are not any pictures or a racy blog post out there that you don't know of. Anything that could hurt your image you need to be concerned about.

Hopefully most of you will not find much to speak of. That is a good thing! If you do find some negative things you should try to do something about it.

If it is a website that posts public records of your arrests you are pretty much screwed. The best you can do is to have everything taken care legally before you move forward. Looming arrests and convictions that are unresolved will defiantly get you shown to the door by most employers. Try and have your business wrapped up as best as possible.

Other sites that have their content posted by individuals may be a bit tricky. For some, you will be able to send an email to the webmaster or administrator. You should be able to just tell them about the slanderous information and ask it to be taken down. Others might not be so helpful. If you are doing the cleanup work on your own just remember to be firm and persistent in your requests to the point of being a pain. If you keep asking they might eventually comply just to make you go away.

There are also additional resources out there for cleaning up a negative image floating around in cyberspace. There are books and web sites along several self help resources that go into great length on the subject.

There are also services that charge a fee to do the removal work for you. If you decide to go that route be sure and know exactly what you want do up front. Be clear and precise with them and make sure they spell out exactly what they will do for you before you pay.

You should also run a background check on yourself before you get started. Almost all of you will try and skip this step. After all, you know that you don't have a criminal record! I see your point but what you don't know about yourself can hurt you the most.

What if someone stole your identity? What if someone you once knew used your name the last time they got arrested? This is the information that might end up on a background check that costs you that new job.

The companies you are applying for jobs at doing those background checks are not normally used to getting back negative information. They do not know who you are so the last thing they will be is understanding in your plight. They have heard before the "I swear I never did that! I don't know how that got on my record!"

I'm sorry to have to tell you this, but if you are put in that position they won't believe you even if it is the Gods honest truth. Now you just lost your shot at that perfect job for something you didn't even do. Well kiddies, it happens all the time. So go take a look at what is out there in your past that you *didn't* do.

Now if you find something, it may or may not be easy to get off your record. Here is a trick: go see a lawyer. I know some of you cringe at the thought, especially considering the cost. But most legal counselors will give you the initial consultation for free. Take your background check to them and that will at least let you know your options and where you stand.

You may find out that it is a viable option as well as affordable to get him to do the work for you. If the first one you talk to won't give you a break then go and get a second opinion. Lawyers are a dime a dozen and they are all competing for your business. Somebody is bound to cut you a deal.

You can also try taking your ID down to the police station with your background check. Every once in a while the police can run your prints and give you instruction on how to take care of things on your end. It's worth a shot.

Whatever you do, make sure you have proof you got it corrected and be up front with your potential employer. By proof I mean legal documents, not a note from your mom as to where you actually were on the night in question. If you can prove it then it won't hinder your chances in the job hunt.

Some of you will breeze through getting the things done in this chapter with no trouble. Good for you! For some it may not be so easy.

I understand it can be a little scary to have to look in your own closet for skeletons. Most of us, me included, would rather leave those bodies where they are buried and forget about them. However I cannot stress enough how important it is to have a clear view of how employers will see you *before* you get started. A little time and effort now could save you a lot of headache in the future.

CHAPTER 2 QUICKIES:

- Clean up your Facebook, MySpace or any other social network sites. Get rid of negative information or things that could be frowned upon by a potential employer.
- Look yourself up on several search engines to see what may be floating around out there that you don't know about.
- Order a background check on yourself to avoid surprises.

Chapter 3

Your Resume

Your resume is nothing more than a tool. As a matter of fact it is a simple tool that has but one purpose. The only intent of your resume should be to get you in the door.

Problems arise when you try to make your resume into some sort of personal promotion flyer about who you are, your dream, and your beliefs. Professionals stick to business so your resume should be all business. You do not want to have your resume try and convey how great of a person you are or how awesome your hobbies are. That is not your resumes purpose. Your resume should be simple, straight forward and relay the three things. You are qualified, you have experience and you are educated—'nuff said. Those are the pillars of what your resume should contain. Don't color outside those lines! Potential employers should review your resume and want to get you in for an interview—period.

First and foremost, you do need a resume. You may have limited experience or limited education, but you do need to have one. More importantly, you will be judged by your resume. Since the only expectation should be for your resume to get you an interview, then you want to be judged positively.

You will never be hired based solely on how great your resume is. But you will be turned down based on how unprofessional your resume is. It's a double standard which is not fair but that is the game. I have seen thousands of resumes and the overwhelming majority of them were garbage—total garbage! They were too long, too short, hard to read, hard to follow, didn't make sense, out of date, out of focus or just plain out of line.

Sending your resume in on bright yellow or pink paper because you think it will help make it stand out is an ultimate fail (in case you were wondering). And if your resume happens to fall into any of those negative categories listed above, it goes right to the rejection pile. What you may not know is that your resume is sitting in a pile of other resumes, probably a big pile. The quickest way a person doing the first sort of those resumes is to whittle them down the easy way. If they look substandard, unorganized, or even in the wrong format you will probably get rejected automatically. Most companies will not really waste the time to read something that is sub-standard. That is just the way the ball bounces. To avoid this you have two options:

Option one: take a class at your local junior college on resume writing. Learn to do it the right way from a real person. You want it to be professional and fit the guidelines that Human Resource folks are looking for. There are standards and it is best you follow them. The templates provided in software packages are good, but they do not teach you much about content or what to put in them. Software program templates are basically how to put a resume together. Content is very important. Too much and you will turn someone off at the idea of even talking to you. Too little and you may not get your interview.

Option two: pay a professional to do it for you.

I recommend option two in all counts. Taking a class will take a lot of time and it is highly likely you will come out of the class not knowing exactly what you are doing. That could cost you a potential job interview. Don't risk it! Pay a professional service to build your resume for you. A resume service can work wonders. They build and create thousands of high quality resumes for all levels of professionals. A resume service will know what it will take for your resume to get you in the door of a perspective employer. Let them work their magic and you will be pleased with the results. Of course this will cost a bit of cash. However, if you are lucky enough to have loving parents I would bet the odds of them paying for it are pretty good. It's worth a shot. Try this:

"Dad, I want to increase my chances of getting a good job. I think I should have a resume service help me with getting my resume together. Would you help me pay for that?"

Now your father may have to pick himself up off the floor from the shock of the intelligent things you have just spouted off. However, I bet if it is within his means what so ever he would jump at the chance to contribute to your success.

Option two is not expensive and it is money well spent. Some professional resume writers will do this for a very low fee, $75 sometimes. There are also a great deal more that are middle of the road on pricing and offer a bit more with their service. Perhaps you might get a consultation, rewrites, edits, and updates; even interviewing tips! My advice is to get the most you can for what you can afford to spend, and if at all possible spend a little more.

Your references will be just as important. Don't just generate a list out of your cell phone when you are filling out an application. Have several personal and professional references ready with all of their correct contact information. Talk to your references *before* you use them. Knowing what they will tell your potential employer will provide you valuable insight.

There is one last thing to remember. Always get your resume in several different formats. More often than not your potential employer will ask for your resume in a certain format: MS Word 2007 or newer, PDF or even a snail mailed hard copy. It is not this way because one is better than the other. It is this way because that potential employer has decided to handle resume in that fashion.

Have your resume ready to go in several different formats. Be ready! Rarely will you be asked to snail mail a regular copy of your resume, but it will happen from time to time. Choose a good quality white paper that you can pick up at your local office supply store. You may be asked to fax in a copy, or perhaps attach it to an email or insert in text format in an ad response form. Most employers only accept certain standards when it comes to resumes and they stick with it. If they want MS Word only formats and you send in a .pdf then odds are you will get deleted. If you have to stop and convert your MS Word 2000 resume to Word '07 you lose time that may cost you an interview. Whatever a potential employer dictates is the format, give them exactly that.

CHAPTER 3 QUICKIES:

- Your resume is only a tool to get you in the door.
- Hire a professional to build your resume for you.
- Be ready to go with your resume in several different formats.

Chapter 4

Big Day Impressions

THAT RESUME HAS PAID OFF and now the big day for your interview is at hand! If you are trying to get on board with a company that is large enough to have a Human Resources department, you need to be aware of first impressions. This will hold true for smaller companies with just an office manager or supervisor as well. You could also interview directly with your future boss, but generally Human Resources get the first—or last—say in hiring you. So their option matters.

When you begin your dealings with the HR department for your interview, there is an important guideline you should keep in mind. It is almost always impossible to really impress someone from HR. However, it is very easy for them to form a negative opinion of you at any point in the interview process. In other words, your interview is not an episode of *Jack Ass*. You will not gain their favor by trying to entertain them.

If you want to make yourself appear in a positive light then be easy to deal with. When that HR person calls to set up your initial interview, stop what you are doing immediately. Engage yourself in the conversation with that person and nothing else. Do not try to talk over the radio or TV on in the background. Turn everything else off! Give the person who is on the phone your undivided attention. When they offer an interview time, accept the first time they give you if at all possible. Do not go back and forth trying to reach a time that is convenient for you! The time should be convenient for them. The only reason you should not be able to come to the interview time they offer is if you have a different interview scheduled during that time frame. The sooner you can interview the better. If you push the time back or put it off till it is convenient for you, they might be swayed by another person that interviewed before you did.

When you arrive for your interview the first thing to do is smile! A frown on your face during the interview makes a bad impression. A good smile says 'pleasant attitude' to your interviewer, so smile! This one factor alone has the potential to make or break an interview. That smile can put you over the top and it will leave a great impression after you finish your interview. If you don't know how stay smiling then plop your butt in front of your mirror and practice. That's right, practice smiling while talking about your accomplishments or education. Yes . . . I'm dead serious. Practice it.

I also want to give you the best piece of advice that might ever come out of this book. If you take one singular thing from this book and apply it to the rest of your entire career, this would be it. 15 minutes early really means you are on time. Arriving at the exact time scheduled really means you are late. So if your interview is at 11:00 then be there at 10:45. That does not mean you hit the parking lot at 10:45; if you do that then you are already late. By 'be there' I mean you have stopped by the restroom and are in the waiting room, checked in, ready to go. If it is a place you have never been then drive there the day before and find it. Time how long it takes you to get there and add 10 minutes to your drive time for every 30 minutes it would normally take you to drive. Be early no matter the cost.

If you have to make the person interviewing you wait for any reason, *any* reason—than you are almost guaranteed certain death. They will convey the following: "Interviewed well—showed up late." If it were a choice between you and the next person whose comments only said "Interviewed well", who do you think they would choose? I have news for you snowflake, there are people who think you are special and unique; the people interviewing you are not those people. They are paid to be judgmental when it comes to anything and everything about you.

There are lots of things that by law they cannot ask in making their evaluations of you, but information offered is graciously accepted. What you say or do can and will be used to evaluate you in a hiring process. The text book questions listed in interview books will be asked in one form or another. It is the information offered by you without them asking which may slight an opinion one way or another. What makes an impression with the person doing the interview may be things you take for granted. Here are a few examples.

You follow HR person to an interview room and you say "let me get that" as you open the door for that person. They will be able to tell you possess good manners; Great impression! You answer questions with 'sir' or 'ma'am' pleasantly. This shows courtesy and respect. Great impression! Do you see where I am going here? I am talking about the things that your mother tried to teach you, but you may have generally ignored. When engaged in a conversation with an interviewer, avoid the use of slang. Slang words are interview killers! If you still find yourself lacking in this area there are several business etiquette books out there that will help you brush up.

Making a good impression goes all the way to the way you smell. Easy on the perfume or cologne is the way to go. If you are a smoker, you will need to ease up or cut out the smoking on the morning of your interview. Get some nicotine gum to tide you over because you will surely be nervous. If you disregard this bit of knowledge and chain smoke before your interview it casts a shadow with your interviewer. Another bad impression is coming in to the interview wearing sunglasses on your head. That makes you look like an idiot! Leave the shades in the car along with that pesky cell phone. Just because you may be going to an interview to be a grocery sacker doesn't mean you don't have to act professional. Wearing that baseball cap does not make you look cool. In fact you look like you have a total lack of respect by showing up to an interview in one. Always keep in mind that it is all about first impressions.

How you dress on the big day will say a lot about you as well. Your attire should always be business professional no matter what. Business professional means no loud colors and crazy outfits. Think of the nicest formal function you can, then apply that to a business setting. Church, weddings, funerals, or graduation ceremonies should be the baseline you use when deciding on business attire. That means slacks with a belt along with a pressed shirt and tie. By all means wear a suit if you own one! Ladies don't let your wardrobe slide on interview day either. Sandals are not appropriate unless you are a lifeguard. Go with the best skirt or blouse you have and you can't go wrong. Business suits for women are very fashionable and stylish by today's standards. An interview is the perfect excuse to go and buy something new! It doesn't matter if you are a girl or a guy you can still be hip and stylish while wearing business attire. If you are unsure of yourself about business attire to suit your style, there are several professional business attire books and websites that will meet your needs. People will judge a book by its cover, and your cover is your clothing. You want to be pressed and dressed on interview day so you can give off the image of a true professional!

CHAPTER 4 QUICKIES:

- Show up early no matter what.
- Easy on the cologne or perfume; cut out the smoking.
- Use good etiquette skills when dealing with people.
- Dress business professional.

Chapter 5

Navigating Your Interview

THE INTERVIEW PROCESS MAY TAKE several twists and turns or go down more than one path. By that I mean that for different companies, one size does not fit all. You could interview once with the person that will be your boss and bang, you got a job! You may have to interview with Human Resources, a company supervisor and then your boss before you get an offer. Sometimes the process will take a day and sometimes it will take a month. I have personally experienced a hiring process that took me almost two months to get through. Companies generally stick with what they know, so don't get frustrated if the process takes longer than you want it to.

Don't get annoying about finding out how you did in your interview. It is very unprofessional to call a potential employer where you interviewed and check to see what the company decided four times in a week. If they want you, they will call. If they don't call then they probably don't want you. You could possibly get a rejection letter, but those are hit or miss. Unless they tell you to call back on a certain date, it's a waiting game.

It doesn't matter who you interview with or how many times, be early to every interview. We have discussed this in the previous chapters, but I cannot stress this enough. Have a little check list when you go out the door to your interview so that you don't get behind schedule. This will help you get ahead of the curve by making sure you have all your bases covered before you get there.

There are other little tips that can make a big difference, like bringing your own pen. I know that sounds ridiculous, but it is the honest truth. You will have to fill out some forms or an actual application. Some HR departments don't provide a pen on purpose. Me personally, if someone showed up to fill out an application without a pen, I wouldn't even talk to them. Some entry level jobs will give you a marker or felt tip pen to fill out the application, that way they know when they look at the application you came unprepared. Bringing a pen simply states you came prepared. Also, have a professional looking leather notebook with you for your interview. Keep copies of your resume and copies of your list of references. You will also want to make sure to have a pad of paper in there to take notes. You should always take notes during an interview.

Before you get to your interview you should be aware of a few other things. The companies will more than likely want to run a background check; we discussed this already. Some will only check for the big felonies while others will pull up every ticket you have ever had in your life. The point is they will definitely look into you. Companies will give you a chance to disclose your background up front before they check. If you know you are clean then no worries. If not, this is will be a test. If you disclose nothing before a background check and they find something, you will immediately be disqualified. You lied, period. That is just the way they will see it. Tell the truth, admit your past mistakes and they will more than likely overlook some things if you interview well. Professionalism means being honest, especially about yourself.

Before you go to each interview, make sure to do some research on the company you are interviewing with. Know as much as you can about what they do before you arrive to your interview. A majority of interviewers will ask you directly what you know about the company. If the company happens to be a service industry company like a restaurant chain, then perhaps you should eat there a few times. Spend considerable time before hand doing background research on the company by looking for information on the web. Get to know them and the areas of their business before you go in for an interview. Professionals do their homework, so when it comes to interviewing with a potential employer you should do your home work and learn about them.

What will be asked of you in your interview? Lots of things and the questions will be all over the board. A lot actually depends on how good the person is interviewing you is. If they are untrained they will be asking you scripted questions and writing down the answers. If your interviewer sits down with you with nothing in front of them, you will be in for a thorough interview. The name of their game is for you to talk more than they do. That is generally what all interviewers want and set out to do. Sometimes you will get lucky and the person interviewing you gets comfortable and starts talking your ear off! If so, let them talk! Listen actively and intently, smile and laugh when appropriate even if you may not find the person funny. If your interviewer likes you, your chances of getting the job will increase dramatically.

A great many Human Resource professionals are just that, strictly professionals. They are all business and their aim is to be good at their business. Their business is finding people like you and hiring the best person for the job. Low turnover rate (the rate at which a company loses employees and has to hire new ones) is a sign of a good HR department. To do their job they have to remain within a strict set of rules. Equal Opportunity Employment leveled the playing field so they can't ask you personal questions. For instance, they might ask if you have transportation to work. Valid question, but what they really want to know is do you have your own car? They can't ask that. So if you ride your bike (which is in fact valid transportation) then your answer is yes. It is the same thing with riding the bus. They will ask if you have transportation, not what your transportation is. So your answer to that question is yes, unless you expect your boss to pick you up for work.

They are not supposed to ask you if you have kids either. Some human resource managers will talk about their own kids or family with the hopes that you will talk about yours. What that means is, they cannot ask you, but if you offer and start blabbing every detail about your personal life they will gladly listen. It then becomes a valid part of the interview because you offered. If you have six kids and you ramble on in the interview about how crazy life is with them, you may be looked at as unreliable because you could have a sick kid all the time and miss work. That is not fair, but that will be the stereotype put on you. Therefore take the kids out of the equation. If your interviewer talks about their family, indulge them in their own stories but share none of your own. If you feel obligated to talk, then share something about a niece or nephew. If you end up dealing with an untrained interviewer they may come out and point blank ask you if you have kids. You can side step that question by saying you have a "happy little family" with a smile on your face. If you are interviewing with a trained professional then your personal life should be out of the discussion.

A quaint little trick is to try and combine the last two topics discussed without actually asking at all. The Human Resource office may be on a floor with a window where they can see outside when you arrive. They take a peek at you and can tell you have transportation because you drove yourself. They can also see that there are no car seats in the car, so you may not have little ones. Some will resort to walking you to your car or touring the property to get a better look. You may even be asked to drive your interviewer to another location, especially if you could be working offsite. You are a professional which means you are smart enough to beat people at their own game! If you take the public transportation system most of the time, drive to your interview. Perhaps your car is a piece of junk and has 2 permanently attached car seats because you do actually have little ones. In that case, take a friend's car or your parents' car. Clean the vehicle out the day before the interview as well. You don't want 3 weeks of trash built up in the floor board just in case the possibility arises that you may have to drive your potential new boss somewhere.

Your previous employer will come up, you can bet on that. You should write down a highlight reel of your previous jobs before you do any interviewing and practice discussing them. The information you relay about each previous employer needs to be the positive highlights. Going into an interview and trash talking your previous employer is very unprofessional. Talk about the all of the accomplishments you made while you were employed there. Now you will get the question of "Why did you leave?" or "What did you not like about working there?" Answer the question positively, which you may have to rehearse in advance. Tell them there was not enough room for advancement or you didn't feel challenged in your former position. If you were a victim of downsizing, it is acceptable to share your disappointment. If you were escorted out of the building by armed guards after being fired, you better have some really creative answers!

One way to help yourself come off very well to your interviewer is to have a list of questions ready for them. This will show you have put some thought and research into your interview. Asking questions at your interview in this manner is very professional! It also gets them to open up more about what you may be doing at that company. You will be able to make a more informed decision about taking the job if you give them some questions to answer. Some good ones I like are:

- What are the company's plans for growth in the future?
- What will the training program be like?
- How does the employee review process works?

Notice those are not "me" questions. Your questions don't all need to be about the money, benefits, and time off. If at the end of the interview you do not have a clear picture of the benefits then ask. Just make sure to ask company focused questions as well.

Navigating your interview from start to finish can be very nerve racking, even for the seasoned professional. There is a lot riding on this potential job and the pressure will get to you. You can prepare for that by taking your interview seriously and putting plenty of thought into it before you go. The better prepared you are, the better off you will be.

CHAPTER 5 QUICKIES:

- Show up early; bring a pen, extra resumes and references.
- Know in advance what will show up in a background check.
- Do some research on every potential employer where you will interview.
- Don't talk trash about your last job in an interview.
- Take notes in your interview.
- Have a list of questions to ask them.

Chapter 6

Closing the Deal

Here it comes, get ready for it. That phone call you have been waiting for. That email in your in box, that letter in the mail. It's a job offer; they want you to come to work for them! You did it! Go ahead and do the happy pee-pee dance for a bit, I'll wait for you.

How you handle that offer is really up to you. Most offers will come with a starting salary based on your interview, your experience and the company pay scale. Some of you will jump on the phone and accept what they offer. There is absolutely nothing wrong with that. It is a commendable decision to just take the money and run. Been there, done that.

Before you call and accept, you may want to examine your own situation. Can you live on this salary? Is the salary comparable to industry average? I only ask those questions because you won't be able ask for more money after you have started. The deal you get is the one you make going in the door. Let me say that again in case you are a speed reader. *The deal you get is the one you make going in the door*. This will be a fact you face throughout your entire career and will never change. You will also come across that piece of information later in the book.

If you accept for five grand under the industry standard then you have to live with it. That does not mean that you should try to negotiate a better deal every time either. Some companies will rescind their offer if you try and negotiate, especially for entry level positions. Take a half day and think about it, make an informed decision—then call and accept. Make sure you see everything from all angles.

Some of you will be in a bit of a different situation in that you have more than one offer on the table and you have to decide between them. This may come down to that old fashioned method in which you write the pros and cons of each on separate pieces of paper and weigh it all out. By all means do that! You can also get help or advice with deciding from someone you absolutely trust. That is a great decision as well. They can look at things more objectively and point a few things out that you may miss. Sometimes other people can look at things and see them in a different light.

You may have a gut feeling telling you which one to pick. One felt better than the other. If that is the case, throw all that other stuff out the window and go with your gut. Just as you made your impressions on your potential employer, they might have made a good impression on you. Always listen to your instinct when it speaks to you. Very rarely will you be let down.

In the end you need to choose what fits your situation best and it doesn't always have to be the money. The location and how it affects your drive time may be something you need to consider. That is another huge factor because the price of fuel is getting out of control. Run the routes on the internet and compare the difference in miles. Do you know what the average MPG is on your vehicle? (Miles Per Gallon) If you are a little lost here, call your dad or uncle. He will be glad to help.

Gas prices are not the only factor when you are talking about distance from work. How long it takes you to get to work can wear on you over time as well. A 30 minute drive may not seem bad for you at first. Look at it this way: 30 minutes a day each way is an hour; times 5 days a week is 5 hours spent driving. That makes a 50 hour work week 55 all of the sudden. That extra time you spend driving gets taken out of your personal time. Less sleep, less personal time, and less family time are things that suffer when you have a longer drive back and forth to work. If you ended up going with a company that was a 10 minute drive each way, that's less than 2 hours each week. When you add the drive time up it may shed some additional light on what the true situation would be, and it is very professional to do so.

You may try and narrow it down to whatever company offers the most money. Perhaps you feel like going back to the negotiating table with both of them and letting them battle it out. If you have the guts enough to do that then go with your bad self! After all, you can't win what you don't put in the middle. My only advice based on my experience here is only go one round with the big boys. Go back to the table and see what they come up with. Once you have done that, pick one—and do it quickly. It is always professional to send an email or letter to the loser of the battle so they know not to expect a call from you. Don't burn any bridges with the company you didn't go with, perhaps you may need to apply again someday.

Companies also have very different benefit packages. If you have 2 separate offers from opposing companies then you may want to call the Human Resource department for each one and discuss benefits. Some companies take very good care of you, some will not. A lot of times in an interview they will tell you that they offer the standard insurance: health, dental, vision and life. What they do not tell you is there is no standard price.

Let's say that 2 separate companies offer you a job, one offers $40,000 and the other $38,000. Most people see the difference of $2000 and go with the highest number. To be thorough, you should investigate further. What you may learn is the first company that offered $40k charges you $70 dollars a week ($3640 a year) and the second company that offered $38k charges $30 a week ($1560 a year). That makes the difference in the cost of the 2 companies' benefits $2080 a year. So after you pay your benefits you are actually making $80 a year less with the company that offered the $40,000! Getting this type of information could tip the scales of your decision between employers.

If it wasn't clear in your interview, find out about time off to help you with your decision. Paid time off (PTO), vacation and sick time vary from one company to the next. Some will offer all three of those and some will only give you one lousy week a year, standard. One week a year is fast becoming obsolete, but it does happen. Lots of companies give you more weeks the longer you are there, which help them remain competitive. Vacation and paid time off should weigh very heavy on which company you choose. Remember, you can avoid burn out by getting much needed time off and well deserved rest. If you need more detailed help on the subject of negotiating with your potential new employer, I recommend doing further research on the subject. There are volumes of information at your disposal to guide you through the negotiation process.

When it comes to the company you ultimately accept employment with, or whatever one accepts you, be firm in your decision. You are starting your journey of being a professional, and you have to start somewhere. The success you desire comes from climbing the ladder one rung at a time—starting generally at the bottom or somewhere close to it. You should be able to remain a steadfast professional within your organization and build your career skills there. Skills learned today at this company may be used at a new company that offers you better opportunities. There will be many factors that influence and affect your career throughout your life. Being a professional is the key to making it all work for you.

Chapter 6 quickies:

- Evaluate your drive time and distance as part of your decision.
- Look at the benefits offered and what they cost you.
- Know how much time off you get and take it regularly.
- Always go with your gut.

Chapter 7

Wearing the Golden Handcuffs

You have survived the whole hiring process and have gotten a great new job, congratulations! No matter what direction or background in life you are coming from you are making the right choice! Believe it or not, by deciding to take on this daunting task of being professional you have actually done what your parents have either been secretly saying they wish you would do—or they have actually said it to your face.

Grow up.

Deciding to do something about your career, or lack thereof, has caused you to just grow up. What you may not realize is you have actually taken the first step. From people on 12 step programs all the way to just normal folks with problems, they have all learned the same thing. That is, at one point or another actually admitting the problem is a huge step forward. By deciding you need to be more professional in your career means you have admitted to yourself that you need to make improvements. Great job!

I need to warn you before we go any further. I implore you to take the time to read these next few paragraphs and take them to heart. You have made the decision to do something about improving your professionalism and I commend you for it. But there is one last decision to make and you are going to have to take it very seriously.

Do you want to wear the golden handcuffs—or not?

Deciding on whether or not to wear the golden handcuffs is a conscience decision and is the next step if you are to move forward from here. Most of you may not know what this means; let me explain.

In any workplace setting, being a professional and having success means you cannot have your cake and eat it too (Sorry . . . I know you are disappointed. But "having your cake and eating it too" is reserved for rock stars and actors). Unless your workplace is a privately held company and you are the sole owner, you have to answer to someone and play by their rules. Now that starts with your first interview at the company and ends on your last day of employment. It may the last day of your life, depending on if the company works you to death! "They" refers to a long list that starts with your boss and goes all the way up to the CEO and shareholders. You will have restrictions in most cases—handcuffs—but they are made out of gold. Gold in that the longer you wear the handcuffs, the better you are at playing by their rules. The more professionally you handle yourself then the more opportunities for advancement, better pay, and promotions will hopefully be afforded you. All of that translates into the gold in the handcuffs I am referring to. But you have to play by the rules and these are rules you don't make. You may not even be allowed an opinion on the rules, even though your opinion may be right.

It's kinda like living with your parents 8 hours a day and getting paid for it.

The rules by which you must play vary slightly from company to company, but they will have striking similarities.

There are a lot of rules which are written down for you and if you are a person that reads the instructions and can follow them, you will fare well. Other rules may not be written down and you will have to learn them the hard way. Of course, by reading this book you are jumping ahead of the learning curve in the "learning things the hard way" segment of being professional. Unfortunately those unwritten rules may still turn your stomach.

This may mean kissing butt.

This may mean being nice to people you wouldn't pour water on if they were on fire.

This may mean doing your job, and someone else's.

This may mean you can't be gangsta from 9 to 5.

Sorry . . . I can see you are disappointed again. It happens.

I will talk a lot about those unwritten rules because you have chosen to wear the golden handcuffs of being professional in the workplace. Following those rules may seem a burden, especially at first. But in the long run it will pay dividends and dollar signs if you do it right.

The rest of this book will address some of the more common unwritten rules you will see in the workplace. These are generally the big ones that everyone will come across at one time or another.

Of course you must also be aware of those unwritten rules that are unique to your particular work environment. Keep a sharp eye out to avoid learning those rules the hard way.

That's it. If you can handle wearing the golden handcuffs that your employer will hand you on the first day of work—you are good. You have already started your mindset of being a professional and you should proceed on to the next chapter. If you can't do it, put the book down, move on and I wish you luck—you'll need it.

If you are still up for the challenge then by all means continue.

CHAPTER 7 QUICKIES:

- Decide now how you will adapt to wearing the golden handcuffs in your profession.
- Know in advance you will have to kiss butt or be nice to people who don't deserve it.
- You may have to adjust you lifestyle choices to suit the workplace environment.
- Watch for unique unwritten rules in your particular work environment.

PART 2

ON THE JOB

So you got the job?! Congratulations!! This section will help guide you through some of the day to day things that are usually taken for granted when trying conduct yourself as a professional. Hopefully you have fared well through the hard part, which is actually getting the job, and now are ready for the next challenge! We are going to look at being a professional sort of "out of the box" in that we will address things separate of your personal life. The distinction between professional and personal sometimes ends up being a grey area.

To put things plainly, you will become 2 people. For those of you that happen to have a few issues, you will add an additional personality to how ever many your mind is currently housing (LOL). This new person is the one you will become when you are at work. This is the professional. Your slacker, lazy ways on your own time are fine and dandy. But when it's time to get down to business you need to be all business.

It starts in the morning as soon as you get up to get ready for the work day. Your focus is to get ready physically and get prepared mentally. It is like psyching yourself out before the big game. Your mental conditioning will become that of a trained boxer getting in the ring. You hype yourself up, get in the middle and put in work, then get out.

The professional, business side of you will be a continuing work in progress and you will get better and better at it. This book teaches you some of the ways of the professional and you should carry those with you. Take the "quickies" from the end of each chapter and read over them before you start your work day. Keep them fresh in your mind as to not forget them. Before long you will find yourself doing things from this book automatically without thinking about them before hand. Now get on the job!

Chapter 8

Showing Up

Y OU HAD BETTER HAVE A game plan for showing up to work. I don't mean on day one, I mean in general. You should have an overall plan of execution when it comes to you being at work. Don't get nervous, I'm going to give you most of the plan.

First and foremost is your first 90 days of employment. Your first three months is a snapshot of you for your new employer of what they can expect overall from you. This is at least as far as attendance and possibly performance is concerned. The reason I say 90 days is this: Some states like Florida or Texas are known as 'right to work states.' This means you can quit your job and not give notice or reason, and the employer can let you go under the same circumstances. An employer exercising that right generally does so in the 90 day probationary period. Look online to see if your state is one of those particular states.

Also at orientation, you may actually have to sign 90 day probationary period papers with your other materials. This signed form is usually reads the same as a states' law for a 90 day probationary period of employment. This basically says your employer has the right to fire you at any time with in the first 90 days and they don't have to tell you why or pay unemployment benefits. Sucks huh!?

With this in mind, your plan for the first 90 days is this: never come in late and never miss a day. Your employer will track your attendance and if on day 85 you have been late twice and missed a day, you might not be worth keeping to them. Keep your time and attendance as punctual and accurate as possible during your probationary period. It is good for your job security and makes you look very reliable and professional.

After your 90 days are up you should show up on time all the time! I know people that are chronically late for everything. If you are one of those people then you will have to go above and beyond here. The first sign of a professional is they are punctual and timely. Remember, being on time means being there before start time. If you are one of those people that end up being inexcusably late all the time your boss will tire very quickly of your excuses. I have personally seen people fired and fired them myself simply because they could not come to work on time. Inexcusable!

Granted, everyone is late now and again. If you are finding yourself running late, call your office manager, boss or the person you report to. Let them know you are late and when—*exactly*—you will be there. Do not *ever* call a coworker and have them tell the boss you will be late. If that coworker drops the ball then you are left holding the bag. Call and speak to the boss and apologize to them when you get there. Try not to let it happen again. What I am saying is your boss doesn't want to hear excuses for why you are late. They want you to fix it and not be late anymore.

People also get sick, which is understandable. Your best bet is to know to the letter what your company expects. This varies widely from company to company so make sure you understand what expectations your employer has set. Some of you extremely lucky few will get actual sick time. Use it wisely and accordingly. Don't burn it up just because it is a nice day outside this spring when you know that you get bronchitis every winter and are down for 2 days. Contact the right person when you are sick and follow the company guidelines.

Have a plan in advance for the times when your kids get unexpectedly sick. Some of you have support systems in place by way of in-laws or grandparents you can call on for help. Get an arrangement lined up with them in advance if you ever need to call them if little Johnny wakes up with a fever. If not, you may have to find another way of arranging care when you have a little one that is sick. Kids get sick, it happens—I understand that completely. I am not trying to be an uncaring hard-ass here. (I have 6 kids of my own, so I feel your pain) What I want to relay to you is your employer may likely be an uncaring hard-ass. They care about the results, the numbers or the bottom line. If you are out sick because of the kids that may affect those bottom line results. So the least amount of work time missed due to the kiddos, the better off you will be. Finally, unless it is the company Christmas party or July 4th cookout, don't ever bring your kids to work because your sitter fell through. Never!

The rest of you will have to pay attention to the actual guidelines your company has established when you are sick. Some employers will require a doctor's note if you call in less than 4 hours before a shift, some will require one no matter what. Whether or not they can actually do that depends on two things, the state you live in or what you signed when you started with the company. If you signed a policy saying you will call within a certain time period before your shift, you are stuck with it no matter what your state law is. This policy you sign will be considered a condition of employment and you have the burden of upholding it. Those are rules.

True professionals know these rules going in and they abide by them. Doing so is good for your career! If you are unable to abide by the rules, they surely won't promote you and expect you to enforce them upon those under you.

I mentioned your job performance earlier in this chapter as well. If you are not cutting it in the first 90 days your new employer will certainly take note of it. Missing the expectation as far as your performance is a lost investment in you as far as the company is concerned. So if you are lagging behind in your job, don't expect to make it past the 90 day mark.

Take advantage of opportunities that present themselves when those who skipped this chapter don't come to work. Granted you salary folks won't make anymore, but the points you score with your boss when you cover for the sick guy are priceless. Professionals are team players and there is no better way to show team than by picking up the slack. Doing this shows 'above and beyond' when it comes to the company and decision makers will eat it up.

The Dallas Mavericks won the NBA Championship while I was writing this book. I am not a basketball fan, but I read the news religiously. In one of the games in the series, Dirk Nowitzki played while he was sick. He had a summer cold, was coughing and had a fever of 101. Members of the opposing team were reported to have made fun of him; the implied accusation was that Dirk was faking it. Dirk remained professional and his team won the series. Boys and girls you can't fake winning. Michael

Jordan did the same thing once. He played in the 1997 series finals with the series tied 2-2. Jordan had possible food poisoning and a stomach virus, combined with dehydration. They won that game for 2 reasons: It was a great team and Jordan, despite being deathly sick, was a professional and took the opposing team to school scoring 38 points. Afterwards they practically had to carry Jordan off the court. Both of the athletes came to work on time despite being sick and picked up the slack for the team. That is a true professionals' motto—team. Winning is an attitude and winning attitudes are held by professionals. Show up at game time with your professional attitude, it will help you win!

CHAPTER 8 QUICKIES:

- Have perfect attendance and performance in the first 90 days.
- Pick up the slack for the team whenever you can.
- Always have a professional, winning attitude.

Chapter 9

The Way You Look

THIS CHAPTER COULD TAKE FOREVER. If I were going to get in the trenches of fashion we may never get out. Rather than do that I will let you battle the fashion bug on your own terms with your own style. We will stick to the highlights that seem to be prevalent in the workplace today.

Let's first discuss your actual person, the physical you. Piercings have become the new trend as of late. Unless you are working at one of those ultra hip types of places, piercings will not be allowed. The more guest centered your company is, the more likely the company stance will be no visible piercings. The issue is that the company is always trying to project *their* image. If your company is going for the all American business look, then visible piercings will not fit with their image. A company may let you keep that extra hole in your face, but you could have to take it out every day before work. Then again, your employers' stance might be *absolutely not*. This means you may have to seriously consider giving up the piercings. There are a few employers that do not have a stance on the issue. If it is left up to you, I would encourage you to consider just giving up on the piercing all together. This of course only applies to those that you can see. Those other "personal" type of piercings you can generally keep with the exception of the tongue piercings. Companies will frown on those as well due to the fact that most of you with a tongue piercing use it as a chew toy, which is unappealing. Sorry, I know those are your feelings I just stepped on.

(*Warning*: I am inserting a wakeup call here, brace yourself!) Getting your feelings stepped on is something you should probably get used to. The business world isn't going to treat you like the special person you have been raised to think you are. Therefore you will need to start becoming more mainstream and less of a unique shining star; at least as far as being a professional is concerned. You will not be told you did a great job when you actually didn't. You will not get a trophy for second place. You are going to have to earn your professional stripes, nobody will ever just hand you any.

That wasn't so bad, was it?

The same applies to visible tattoos. Now if you were smart when you got it, then your tattoo is probably in a place where it is not visible. If you are "sleeved up" on both arms, you may be able to slide by if you are wearing long sleeves all the time. Other visible tattoos, such as those on the hands or above the neck line will have to be covered. This can be done with bandages or make up which could get costly over time. Your employer may or may not allow the cover up, but they will tell you that up front or as soon as they see it.

Guys will usually have to abide by strict facial hair policies. Do not ever come to work without having shaved. You are not Brad Pitt and you do not look cool, you look like an unprofessional slob. That day you let it slide and do not shave will be the day the boss wants to have an impromptu meeting. You must shave every day, period.

Wrist bands are another thing that seems to be in style, but sometimes say much more than intended. I see the point and there is nothing wrong with supporting all the worthy causes they promote. *I LOVE BOOBIES*, although supporting breast cancer research is a good cause, is not one of those phrases that make you look professional. You may have your button up long sleeve shirt on but someone, more than likely the wrong someone, will see that wrist band. Take it off before the Vice President of your division, who is a Sunday school teacher, sees it. Believe it or not, the term "boobies" offend a great many people. Having that wording around your wrist is bad for your professional image. Wear it on the weekends with your street clothes.

If you happen to be brave enough to go to a club on a work night, make sure you get the entire hand stamp off the top of your hand too. Evidence of the party the night before work is not a good thing. Showing up smelling of booze looking like you have had a rough night makes you look extremely unprofessional. Furthermore, office party girl is not the secret title you want to have put on you.

On to your clothing! If you wear a uniform everyday to the workplace you will have less to worry about than others. Make sure your uniform is cleaned and pressed. If you can't afford that, buy an iron and learn how to use it. That uniform probably has the company name and logo on it, so you must look professional whenever you wear it. Remember not to wear the uniform to other places when you get off of work. That portrays a bad image of you and the company, especially when you get wheeled out of the local strip club at 2:00am wearing it! This even goes for a company logoed hat.

Lots of companies have gone with relaxed Fridays and you should participate. Wear jeans if that is the Friday dress code, but no jeans with holes. (Yes, they do sell them without holes in them.) Along with jeans, the company may have a more relaxed stance on footwear. You should wear a casual shoe, not running shoes or sneakers. Stick with a causal polo style shirt or basic button up oxford or blouse. No t-shirts unless it is a company provided t-shirt. If it is t-shirt day then for goodness sake put on a belt and tuck the thing in! Tucking in your shirt makes you look professional, so you need to do it! Most business causal shirts for men are designed to be worn tucked in. Ladies can get away with un-tucked shirts more often than not because most blouses are designed that way. Sorry fellas!

Cargo pants, half pants or Capri pants—pants that come down to your mid calf—are not professional. Wear them to the company picnic but not to the office. It is sloppy looking, even if you have the attractive legs to put in them. I understand that those pants and a cheap pair of flip flops are comfortable, but it is not professional at all! If we really wanted to tell the truth here, you are probably not wearing them because of comfort. You probably wear them because you are too lazy to put on real cloths. Be professional, dress professionally.

I am gonna beat this dead horse for a minute: please, *please* do not wear flop flops to work. Show a little bit more professionalism than that will you? Flip flops are not business casual. I don't care if they have sparkles and cost you $50 bucks, *do not wear them*. Flip flops belong on the beach or perhaps a lazy Saturday. They are to be worn on your off time only.

Speaking of shoes, guys you need to pay a little better attention to them. Since we were little boys playing in the mud we have always been hard on shoes. Women never tear up dress shoes! A woman will keep them in good condition as long as they remain stylish. Guys will wear holes in the bottom of a pair of shoes and never replace them. For most men this trait is in our DNA and I have no idea why. You should at least have a black pair and a brown pair of casual dress shoes. Keep them nice and buy a shoe polish kit. Keep them polished so you can tell what color they actually are. When they wear out, throw them out! Lastly, in case you were wondering, brown belts go better with the brown shoes; same with a black belt and black shoes.

Again I will mention the whole ironing thing. I realize that dry cleaning is expensive. Sending a weeks' worth of cloths to the cleaners can start to add up. If you are lazy, like me, you do it anyway. One of the things I have seen done to reduce that expense is to buy cotton/poly blend pants that are wrinkle free. Wash them, throw them in the dryer, and then hang them up instead letting them sit in there overnight. This will generally keep the pants looking good. Shirts are usually much cheaper to have cleaned and starched. If you have patience and time you can iron your cloths yourself and save the money. The point is, do *something*! Coming to work in clothes that look like you slept in them is unprofessional. Do without the wrinkles.

The best thing to do when it comes to how you look is to always go professional. Don't go with the lowest standard of what your company requires you to wear. Dress up, not down. Professional attire says something about you. Guys you should look sharp, not sloppy. Ladies should look smart and stylish, not slutty and overly sexy. What you project with your attire actually is a dual image that you portray. One is of your own sense of style and the other of the company itself. The company is concerned about its image, so you should be concerned about yours.

CHAPTER 9 QUICKIES:

- No jeans with holes. No wrist bands.
- No flip flops!
- Guys need to shave every day.
- Your work clothing should be cleaned or ironed to avoid the wrinkles.

Chapter 10

Social Media Pitfalls

We all have secrets. We all have personal information that we don't want to share with the whole world. As the years have passed, the amount of what is out there in cyberspace on each and every one of us has grown almost to the point of being out of control. You can jump on your computer and find out almost anything about anybody if you really wanted to. Those embarrassing things that we wish would just go away are hanging around out there; its form changed to a digital skeleton in our preverbal closet. But the door is only shut, not locked. Anybody can open the door and that's scary.

For the most part we tend to make things hard on ourselves at our own hand. Facebook, MySpace, and Twitter are just some of the tools we use to practically destroy ourselves. This list of tools is endless. If you think about it, all of those sites really don't serve much of a purpose. Sure you can "stay connected" with your family and friends. But don't you actually talk to those family and friends anyway? Don't you text constantly to most or all of those folks? I guess if you were someone whose family and friends lived in China you could have a valid use for the social networking scene. The rest of us don't really have an actual use for social networking unless you count making your own life more difficult. We get bored and entertain ourselves by showing constant attention to our social networking sites. For some reason we think it is okay to just throw information out there for the entire world to see and we call in social networking.

There is no place in the professional world for personal social networking. You need to cut out all of that nonsense immediately if you plan on getting or keeping a good job.

Now don't get all worked up here because I'm not saying dump your Facebook and MySpace page. Since we have discussed this in a previous chapter, your social network sites should be cleaned up already. Moving forward I am saying is don't air your dirty laundry out every time you log on. For goodness sake stop acting like you life is *The Truman Show*. You may think it is cute, funny, or cool. It is funny and cute to your friends; hell it's funny to me too. But it is all about how it looks to people who don't know you and how funny you are when you are drunk—and it looks *bad*. I know you are in your youth and the youthful love to party! I say party on, but remain professional when you do so. Always remember that people are watching. Keep the things off of your social networking sites that can do damage to your professional reputation.

Don't post how stoned you got last night on your wall.

Don't put pictures of your 'slutty school girl outfit' on your page.

Don't 'like' the Movement to Legalize Marijuana.

Don't put your dream job is a porno star.

Don't tweet you can't remember the person's name laying next to you from last night.

Know what the number one cause of break ups in America is? Facebook. People lose jobs, get arrested, go to prison, get taken off probation, get convicted, lose marriages, girlfriends, boyfriends, and regular friends all because someone posted too much information on Facebook. Now the statistics on job dismissal or failure to hire will never be tracked. That is because companies are not going to readily admit that they didn't give you a job or fired you because of your Facebook wall, but I assure you—*it happens every day.*

You will have to temper what you put on all those social networking sites. Perhaps you have a bad day at work and post on your Facebook wall "My job sucks and my boss is a major jerk"! You might as well have marched down to his office and told him to his face. At least that way you would have gotten the satisfaction of saying it before they fire you.

Yes they can fire you. They can do whatever they want. In some right to work states they do not even need a reason. Calling your boss a jerk on a public social network site will get your butt canned for sure. Guess what genius? Everyone already talks in secret about how they feel about the workplace hottie. Post it on your Facebook, even if your profile is private, odds are that person will hear about it. When they find out about it and complain to the boss they will send you packing before you know what hits you. That's sexual harassment and even CEO's of Fortune 500 companies get fired for that nonsense. Only difference between them and you is they get a couple million bucks to leave, you won't even get paid through the end of the week.

There is a new movement going on out there. Perhaps you have heard of it? It seems to have been started by people like you who are becoming professionals as well as those who are concerned about privacy rights.

The phenomenon seems to be that people are quitting MySpace and Facebook in droves. I know that probably shocks the crap out of you, but it is happening. There is actually a quit Facebook day out there and a website (*www.quitfacebook.com*). A large number of my colleagues and friends, including myself, have given up on their social networking sites as well. That's right, we are quitting cold turkey! The whole social networking scene has just lost its appeal for some of us. If you are really serious about being professional, I would advise you to try giving it up. You will get some strange looks when people find out you gave up your MySpace and Facebook accounts. You will be safe in that if you go out and tie one on at the club this weekend it will hopefully stay between you and the people you were with. Drunken tweets and posts are a dangerous thing.

There is another advantage to not having a Facebook or MySpace page that will help you tremendously as a professional. There will be several points throughout this book that guide you through some of the political traps of being professional. Your Facebook and MySpace page can be a political trap. At the workplace, you want to treat everyone the same. The fact that you are able to treat everyone equally this will show you are ready to manage other people. You have to be consistent with those in the workplace if you are to be affective. How does it look if you accept a friend request of the person next to you, but not the person next to them? Now you are playing favorites and you are doing it publically! This will be a terrible mistake for your professional career! So you see, if you don't have a Facebook or MySpace pages then you never have to worry about what friend requests you accept or reject. If you are not able to muster up the strength to quit your Facebook or MySpace just yet, then make it a rule to never accept friend requests from those you work with.

Most companies will have your computer locked so that you cannot access social networking sites from the office. It is a productivity killer and companies are zeroing in on it. If not, you still should not be using your business computer for anything other than business. Chances are the sites you visit on your work station will be tracked by someone and reported up the ladder to your superiors. It would be best if you just concentrate on being professional at work and surf the web from home.

Back in the old days (rotfl!), things were easier. You put on a suit and tie or heels and a skirt and went to work. You did your job and things remained much simpler: work stayed at work and your personal life stayed at home. That meant you could just be who you wanted at home and not worry about your boss finding out. It worked well because those two sides very rarely crossed paths, if ever. In today's world, largely due to social networking, the work and social lives of people wanting to be professionals are bleeding over on to each other. It's making a horrible mess. The two are like oil and water and are not supposed to mix. Most of the things we do in the privacy of our homes and on our off time were meant to remain private. If something you are doing may do damage to your reputation as a professional you should at least try and refrain from doing it in public—or at least keep yourself form posting it on the web. Some of you do this anyway and you are playing with fire. I highly advise against it.

CHAPTER 10 QUICKIES:

- Google yourself to see what is out there.
- Clean up your Facebook and MySpace or delete them all together.
- Try not to have Facebook friends from work.
- Evaluate how you portray your own image objectively and make changes.

Chapter 11

Cell Phones

FOR MOST OF US OUR cell phones are a necessity. Some of us can't go anywhere without them, not even to the bathroom! They are more than just an innovative piece of technology. They have become an extension of our personality. Your new workplace and the role of being a professional may require you to alter your cell phone habits—and that might take some getting used to.

A cell phone policy will generally be unique to each company. Someone long ago decided what the cell phone policy for your company will be and that has pretty much been the stance ever since. Don't look for it to change anytime soon, companies will generally stick with what works for them.

First things first, go find out what the policy is. More than likely during your orientation on day one with your new company they told you up front. If you happened to get on with a company that just threw you a copy of the employee handbook, now is the time to dig it out and look it up.

There are the extremes, which are the companies that say no cell phones at all. They don't even want to see them out or on your person. These companies generally have this stance because of where they stand on customer service.

If you are in an industry that requires constant and close interaction with customers or guests, you can expect no cell phones to be the standard operating procedure. This will be tough on most of you. The best thing to do is treat cell phone use like smoking. Don't pull it out unless you are 20 feet away from the building. Don't try and sneak a text from your pocket and please don't think you can get away with it by hiding out in the bathroom. If you boss catches you in the bathroom then you have just made twice the trouble for yourself. If you work for one of these strict companies, leave the phone in the car. Check it on your breaks and at lunch. If folks need to really speak to you then give them the office number. However, be aware that too many personal phone calls will get you in a hot spot as well.

Lots of companies will be very vague on the cell phone stance. They will let you carry it on your person and may not think anything of it. This is especially true at corporate facilities because many people are issued company paid cells phones. If you have a company paid cell phone, you should be careful as to what goes in them. You can usually put apps and music on them at your own expense. The camera is also there for you to use as well. Just be aware that everything on that phone the company technically owns. It is company property, so if you take some "racy" pictures one evening on your time off, the company may end up with those pictures and could cause you quite an embarrassment. People sometimes take those pictures and forget they happen to be on the phone. Then months later the phone breaks or needs service and you take it to your IT department to let them handle it. Now the IT guys have naked pictures of your girlfriend; not cool.

If it happens that your company allows cell phone use on property, then etiquette is the rule of thumb here. First, turn the ringer off! Hearing it ding every time you get a text or email will start to get annoying very quickly. You co-workers don't want to hear it and I can assure you neither will your boss. Make sure your phone is on silent without vibrating when you go in to a closed door meeting as well. Folks in the meeting will be able to hear the phone vibrate sitting next to you, and you don't want to be a distraction in a meeting.

Next, never send updates or tweets from work, *never*. Your status and update pages on all of your social networking sites should show absolutely no activity during work hours. A well run Human Resource team will monitor this activity and report your lack or productivity to your boss. This could land you in some hot water, so refrain at all costs.

Make sure to use your phone sparingly and with no exposure to the folks you work with. Today's generation has a bad habit of ignoring the person they are sitting in front of and texting someone else. This is rude and a sign of bad professional etiquette! Doing this will put you in a self-imposed negative light and people will turn sour of you. You are at work, so be in the moment at work. When you get a text, wait till you are alone and have a free moment to respond. Very rarely is something that urgent in which you have to be rude and answer a text. If it is urgent then the person should call you directly. If it is an emergency or expected call, excuse yourself from the person you are with and take the call in private. Don't have a conversation with someone else while sitting in front of another person. Always remain professional.

Give your cell number out as sparingly as possible. If it is a company phone then it will be in the company directory. But if your mom calls you 10 times a day your employer may frown upon that. Remember, just because it is free for you does not mean there is not a bill for someone to pay.

Same goes with text messages. Just because you scored a company phone doesn't mean it is a free ride on the cell phone use. You might want to consider keeping your personal cell phone and keeping your calls separate when on you're off time.

Cell phone use in today's work place is tricky. You will have to actively manage your cell phone use and stay on top of the companies' expectation regarding cell phones.

CHAPTER 11 QUICKIES:

- Know your company's cell phone policy and follow it.
- Never update social pages from work, even on your phone.
- Leave your phone in the car or use it sparingly while at work.
- Turn your phone all the way off during meetings.
- Do not text on your phone while talking to someone in front of you.

Chapter 12

Hostile Work Environment

A HOSTILE WORK ENVIRONMENT IS a complex situation. In its basic form, it means there is discriminatory conduct or behavior in the workplace that is unwelcome and offensive to an employee. That can be towards an individual or a group of people that are a protected class (like women). This can be in many forms, not just one that is sexual in nature. Your aim as a professional should be to not involve yourself at all or be engaged in any such conduct what so ever. Also, you never want to create a hostile work environment or allow it to continue in the workplace. Not ever.

That means if you do something offensive directly or indirectly towards anyone you can get in serious trouble for it. That is a pretty broad field. That is not just restricted to what a person says. It can also be what you do in a physical gesture (i.e. flipping someone "the bird") or degrading pictures around your work area (like a swimsuit calendar). Basically this takes the issue of sexual harassment to another level. Hopefully you are aware that sexual harassment has many forms. Grabbing someone you work with between the legs is defiantly sexual harassment. Your boss asking you to sleep with him for a "leg up" is sexual harassment. Those examples can be easy to see because they are blunt.

A hostile work environment works off of implied meaning. You did something that was totally harmless in your eyes because you weren't trying to do anything wrong. The other person was offended. You just created a hostile work environment. Let's look at an example.

You give the person next to you a little shoulder massage because they said their neck hurts. They may or may not have asked you to, you just did it. They go to Human Resources and complain because you touched them and it made them uncomfortable. That is border line sexual harassment and defiantly a hostile work environment. This example can go farther than that I am afraid. Let's say same example, same situation. The person you gave the massage to loved it, oooh'd and aah'd and felt really relaxed. The person you massaged is attractive, while the person next to them is not. The person next to them is a person of high moral standards and what you have just done made them uncomfortable. The person you didn't even touch goes to Human Resources and complains because what you did created a hostile work environment. That is because you did something that may be implied as offensive and it made them uncomfortable.

The office joke of the day can create a hostile work environment just as easily. Your buddy telling the joke of how the donkey tried to date a drunken squirrel is hilarious to you! Who wouldn't think that was funny!? Well the person in the cubicle around the corner that can hear you talking is offended. They don't talk about things like that and both you and your friend are guilty of creating a hostile work environment. You have to watch what you say around other people. If you want to remain employed at your company, keep the talk to business. Small talk about the weather and sports is generally not offending. However, the 10 minute discussion about the sexy cheerleaders on TV during the game will be off limits. I am sorry folks, but we live in a politically correct age and we all have to learn to navigate ourselves in it.

A hostile work environment can be created even by touching someone else uninvited. Shaking hands is a professional act, you are safe there. Hugging the woman who is a total stranger at a business meet and greet is off limits. Unfortunately the girls generally get away with it. Sorry guys, this is another one of those girls club things, you do not get to hug anyone! If you find yourself confronted with a woman who is a serial hugger, stick your hand out and head her off. Personal space is meant to be just that in a professional setting, personal and off limits.

You may think that sending that funny email to just your one friend at the office is okay. Well I am sorry it is not. Most office set ups send all of your email through a server. That server scans every single word in the email and filters it. It picks up on profanity, vulgarity, negative slang and words that imply violence. If one of those words shows up that email is pulled off the server and goes to someone in charge. Your boss will find out and so will someone from Human Resources. Depending on what that email says can make your punishment range from a talking to or all the way up to being terminated. Keep your email correspondence professional at all costs.

I also mentioned that you can be guilty if you let a hostile work environment go on. This will go against some of your better judgments. Most of you think that if it does not include you and you are not participating then you are off the hook. They were telling the racial joke, not you; you didn't even laugh. However, when it comes out that you are letting that happen and saying nothing then you will share in the blame. As you move into positions of leadership you will be responsible for what others do. If you let something like that go on then it will look bad on you. If you are unsure of how to handle these situations should they arise, consult your HR manager. They will be happy to talk to you about what to do and how to prevent it.

I have another piece of advice for those of you who are truly serious about being professional. Take a sexual harassment awareness or hostile work environment training class. These will be extremely beneficial in your career and help you advance into positions of leadership. Some companies will have their own classes and teach their employees themselves. Others will encourage you to take classes by paying for the class with company funds. These training classes look great on your resume as well. Being a professional is something that is built over time, and this training will be a great building block for you.

CHAPTER 12 QUICKIES:

- Be aware as to what you say or do so that it does not create a hostile work environment.
- Remember, you may not offend the person you are actually talking to. However you may offend the person that you do not know is listening.
- Don't take part in the bad jokes and emails that circulate around the office.
- Take a sexual harassment or hostile work environment course.

CHAPTER 13

OFFICE GOSSIP

THE WATER COOLER GOSSIP IS thick around any workplace now days. If the break room walls could talk there would be overwhelming problems! Gossip is like pancake syrup. When you first get into it, the taste and texture is sweet and kind of fun. However when you are done and try to continue on as normal, the stickiness won't come off. Now you need a bath to get the grime off. Gossip is something that will never be gotten rid of so you will need to know how to get through the muck without getting too sticky.

I feel that the best thing to do in this chapter is to really define what we are talking about first. There are some that think the term gossip means it is limited to the female gender. That is presumptuous and completely wrong. Guys talk smack or gossip just like the girls do. Gossip, in its basic form, is any type of communication in the workplace that is not work related, excluding mundane things like the weather. It also doesn't have to be talk about those that actually work there either. Gossip includes talking about people behind their back in a negative or condescending tone without said person there to defend themselves. Everyone does it so we are all guilty of gossip from time to time.

I am sure if you have picked up on the tone of the book, what you really should do is just keep your mouth shut. Anything that you would not say to the person's face does not need to be said at all. That includes saying something in an email to someone that works outside the company or in the cubicle next to you. Also be aware that if you are venting to your spouse on the phone that more than likely someone can hear you. When in doubt, don't say anything.

A good plan of action is to find your inner circle within your workplace. Hopefully there will be one or two people that you have figured out you can trust. Those are usually the ones that don't have a lot of friends because they are not there to make friends. It is also likely that they have been around for some time and are aware of the pitfalls and problem areas and know how to avoid them. These rare people are good associates to have. If you limit your gossip or company conspiracy theories to sharing with just those folks, you will be much better off.

Of course you will from time to time find yourself in a situation where someone is running their mouth when they shouldn't be and you can't get away. The people that do those types of things are usually the ones that have nothing to lose or they are too stupid to realize what they are doing. Either way they are not someone you want to associate with on any kind of a regular basis. Steer clear of them because more than likely they will be known for starting trouble, and you don't want the bosses to think you are part of that persons group. Professionals realize they have an image to maintain. Trouble makers and the gossip artists are bad for ones image.

A good rule to go with is to listen twice as much as you speak. Don't bring the talk to the table, but if someone does you can listen a bit to see if there is anything to be heard from it. Now and again, gossip will come in and contain useful pieces of information. This is especially true when it comes to who may be on their way out of the company. Knowing in advance who may be leaving helps with positioning yourself to take over that person's job if it is a step up for you.

Be warned however that the word on the streets at the workplace can get you in hot water. This can be the case when the gossip is about another employee. If that person gets wind that so-and-so was saying bad things and spreading rumors, you could be called to the mat on it. You don't need blemishes on your record and your professional reputation just because of a stupid rumor and someone got their feelings hurt. If it happens to be that the talk is about whom so-and-so is sleeping with at the office, run away!

Be wary of the passing bathroom conversations as well. You may be able to swear that no one is in the next stall, but you could be wrong. If the office pot-stirrer starts in about how much of a jerk the boss is for no reason, keep your mouth shut. Nod them off or just flat ignore them. Someone could be listening in the back stall and likely will be someone you don't want hearing that type of talk. There could also be a person halfway in the door that catches just enough of the gripe session to land both of you in hot water. Don't air any dirty laundry in the workplace bathroom, it's bad for business.

Finally, I want to make you aware of an uncomfortable situation you may be put in at some point in your career. Should you choose to get yourself in the middle of all the juicy rumors about anyone and everyone, your boss may question you about it. Even worse, the human resources or legal department may question you about it. For example, there may be talk that Supervisor A is fooling around with Employee B. No one has any proof but everyone is suspicious and the rumor mill is amuck. Then without warning, Employee B quits the company, gets an attorney and sues the company for sexual harassment. Now you have to go in for a deposition. (Note the dark cloud approaching on your horizon.) Were you aware of the rumors surrounding this situation? Yes. Did you report any possibly inappropriate behavior that is against company policy to human resources? No. How does that make you look? Lie about the questions and everyone else tells the truth, then you just lied in your deposition. Either way doesn't look too good for your future at the company. However if you are not involved in all the talk then the situation is completely different. If you don't help spread the rumor mill and you are not involved in the gossip your answers would be different. They would also be the truth. Were you aware of the situation? No. You are in the clear, and still employed I might add.

Granted, the previous example is extreme but it does happen. More importantly, when the gossip runs amuck in a company people get hurt. Have you ever been the one that got made fun of? Have you ever been the one that the entire in crowd talked about behind your back but you still knew they did it? What did that feel like . . . hurts, don't it? Exactly; the emotional damage people do by gossiping about each other far outweighs any other damage. That fact alone should be enough to make you act like a professional.

Best case scenario for office gossip is to remain professional and avoid it. A true professional is there to work, not to gossip. If you are immersed in what you are doing then you won't end up having time for the gossip crap. Leave that stuff to the people you will leave behind when you move up in the company!

CHAPTER 13 QUICKIES:

- If at all possible keep your mouth shut.
- Find 1 or 2 people you can confide in at work if you need to.
- Don't participate in unsolicited discussion and gossip about other people.

Chapter 14

Happy Hour & Dating

" **I** NEED A DRINK. IT'S beer-thirty. Margaretville here I come! You want to grab a cold one?"

You will most defiantly get those questions or something like it sooner or later in your beloved place of employment. A nice, cool alcoholic beverage after work is the backbone of most companies. There is nothing wrong with it, and most of the time it is a good way for the cooped up 9 to 5 crowd to blow off a little steam. It is really fun for the crowd working the not so typical hours! Getting off at ten o'clock and the sun being down has your biological clock set to party! Shorter time frames in the late night makes some of you drink faster so you can get more drinking done. All of that can lead to a slippery slope and you need to be aware of the pitfalls.

"Damn it this guy is shooting down all the fun!!" I am certain some of you are most undoubtedly thinking those exact words. Don't throw the book away yet, I'm not going to kill the idea of having a beer with your co-workers. Having drinks after the work day is done can be a political move sometimes. You want to be invited for a drink, that's a good thing. But you should want a bit more than getting invited for pitcher beer with the mailroom guys all the time.

What you really want is for your boss to invite you out for a couple glasses of wine so he can pick your brain. Company spending accounts were invented for such a thing. Strategy, expectations and company goals have long been mulled over by those select few movers-and-shakers sitting around having drinks. You being one of those people would be a really good thing!

Now if your boss is a 50 year old man and you happen to be a single 22 year old female that's a bad thing. You may be in for some trouble by accepting those types of offers. These types of situations can be a career killer. Now you may very well go and it may end up he is actually picking your brain to hear your ideas for the next big project or thoughts on tomorrow's meeting. It may actually be a completely harmless and very a professional situation. But how does it look?

Think of that 22 year old girl in the cubicle next to you. What if you walked into your local watering hole and saw your boss sitting there with her. What would you think?

Exactly, and you don't want to be that girl.

If your boss is female and so are you—safe. Guys if your male boss takes you out for a beer—safe. Mixed company? Heck no, don't go! The boss may take a group of you, defined as 2 or more plus your boss, out for drinks as a celebration for a job well done or after an exceptionally long hard week. That's great, you deserve that! By all means go and have a few nice glasses of wine or a cocktail on the company dime. That's why your boss has an expense account!

Now for the bad news: I stated you should have a few drinks and that means no more than 2. I know, I know—you can drink 2 drinks standing on your head at 10am. That's not the point. It's not about how much you can drink, it's about how much you *should* drink—and you should only drink 2 drinks. Anymore than that and people may get the wrong impression of you, especially your boss. Plus, once you get more than 2 in you things could get out of hand—fast! If that happens then you are shooting yourself in the foot with your career, at least with that company.

Just a friendly reminder to those of you who do drink; drinks do not go with lunch. Never have a beer or a glass of wine with your meal, not even just one. Having a cold one is a very unprofessional choice. Don't bother trying the whole vodka route because someone may smell it anyway or find out. Being caught after you have had a drink at lunch may cost you dearly, including your job.

Let's say you have a glass of wine with lunch and go back to work, just fine and dandy. Then you happen to fall down the stairs, or even get pushed accidently. Accidents do happen and they are a part of every work place. Wanna know a little secret? More than likely your employer has a policy in place that states if you are hurt on the job, the first thing they will do at the hospital or clinic is drug test you. Any amount of alcohol in your system means you fail, you're fired—no job and you pick up the medical bills. It is all perfectly legal. Plus you will never get any unemployment after you get fired either. As you can see, drinking on your lunch break is a lose-lose situation.

You should also be aware of what some companies deem as a "no fraternization policy". In general, this states that a supervisor for the company can not under any circumstances have drinks or do anything socially with someone lower in ranks. Supervisors cannot hang out with regular employees. The only event supervisors and employees can both attend at the same time would be company sponsored event. Any other social circumstance, even if it is accidental, you will need to avoid at all costs. That means you hit a bar for a solo drink after work and an employee that works under you is already there then you have to leave. I know that really sucks but the companies that enforce these rules are very strict about them. If your company finds out, one if not both of you will lose their job.

What to do about the stunner that has caught your eye at work? These are waters that are very tricky to navigate if you are smitten, so be careful.

Best advice is to stay away from it. Workplace romance can make things very uncomfortable for your co-workers, distract you from your job or can even get you fired. Your work environment will turn south real quick should the romance go sour. So at some point you will have to think with your head and not your heart. (Or the other parts of your body that does the thinking.)

The two of you will probably say to each other in the throes of love that you will keep the relationship separate from your work life and not let your love interfere. That may work if you happen to work for the same company but not in the same building, but only for so long. You may think you are doing a great job at disguising your feelings for one another, however people will catch on. To avoid any issues with your job or gossip amongst your co-workers, you'll need to do more.

I must briefly say that I assume this is a consented relationship between two single adults. If your romance is really a fling, one of you is married, or there is job related pressure coming from one of you being in charge of the other, you will need more than this book. Talk to your family, best friend, priest, pastor, or professional counselor. In the end, relationships that form under those circumstances cost jobs, marriages and much more. Do something and do it fast, you are on the edge of throwing your whole life away.

The most important thing to know is where your company stands on the issue. Almost all companies have written policy regarding this topic, so find out what your company wants you to do. Whatever it is if you have any intention of holding on to the job or the relationship, you have to follow their rule to the letter.

Be prepared for this. It could mean one of you has to leave the company. One of you may have to transfer. This will be very tough and most new relationships won't survive this. Whoever has to leave their job for the sake of the other may lead to the possibility of resentment in the future. Try and hide it and you run the risk of it not working out and the relationship ends while you both are still employed at the same place. Ever work with an ex-boyfriend or girlfriend? That is not a pretty site and I am sure you don't want to be involved in a mess of such epic proportions. Some companies will allow a relationship to continue under strict circumstances. You may have to transfer departments or work in another division. It may be allowed as long as one of you is not supervising the other. If the company does allow it then there is usually written policy addressing such issues.

Lastly, do not put off addressing this no matter what. A great deal of companies today will have an up to date, even stricter policy. It may state that you have 30 days to come forward to the company about the relationship to work out an arrangement. After that, if the company finds out you hid the relationship and the 30 days goes past you both get fired. This is in place to avoid sexual harassment suits if your relationship goes bad in 6 months. Honesty is the best policy in these instances and do so quickly.

CHAPTER 14 QUICKIES:

- Never have drinks at lunch.
- Only have 2 drinks when you are out with colleagues.
- Never go mixed company unless there are 3 or more people.
- Avoid workplace romance or follow company policy when doing so.

CHAPTER 15

IF THINGS GO SOUTH

THERE MAY COME A TIME when you think your future is not so bright at the company you are working for. You might be getting perused by another company looking for talent and you think it is time to leave. Maybe you cannot see the light at the end of the tunnel of your efforts at this company and you feel it is time to move on to bigger and better things. It happens at some point in everyone's career and your intuitions about your job may be right. Here is what you may want to do if you decide to peruse those notions.

First things first, don't start slacking. Cross every *T* and dot every *I* with everything you are responsible for doing. When it comes out you are leaving, you want the company to regret your departure. There have been cases that when faced with the departure of a valuable employee, the company counters and throws money at the person in order to get them to stay. That wouldn't be a bad thing, would it? It is something to consider if it ends up being offered to you. However, don't think about trying to do this to extort a raise out of your boss, it will likely backfire on you.

Also, make sure you are lined out before you jump off your companies' wagon. You should always turn in at least a 2 weeks' notice, a month if you can swing it. That is the professional thing to do and you are in fact a professional! By lined out I mean you have signed and accepted with the new company you plan on going with. The reason you need to make sure of this is that some companies, after receiving official notice of your intent to leave will show you to the door. That's right, you stroll in on Friday to give your months notice and they may tell you to not come back on Monday. Are you sure you have that other job? I hope so.

When working through the logistics of your departure you should keep it professional. If your company has a Human Resources department then you should only deal with them. If not, deal with your boss directly. You will want to give you notice in writing and be ready for whatever they may throw at you next as far as staying or going. Be professional, courteous and don't show any animosity.

"I really enjoy working here but I have found a more challenging opportunity that suits my desire for growth more appropriately." That's all you need to say and you have my permission to use that exact statement if you like, be my guest. If you have given your notice and your company accepted then decides to let you work the time out, you should be obligated as a professional to do exactly that. Work the whole two weeks, show up every day on time and work all the way up until the last day. Keep the same bright and shiny attitude you have always had each and every day all the way up till the end. It shows the sign of true class within you.

Keep the gossip out of the office too. As soon as people find out you are leaving half of them will want to know where and if that place has any more openings. Unless you trust someone distinctly and you absolutely think you will never return to that company, don't try to get anyone else a job where you are going. Other people jumping ship behind you leaves the black mark on your reputation. If it turns out they wanted to return to their former company, all they have to do is lie about you and say you really were the bad influence to leave. The company may buy that because they are already mad that you stole those people away. I know that is not what you did, but that is how it will be viewed. If you wanted to come back to the company but you took people with you, they more than likely not allow you to return. Knowing all that, it will be in your benefit to keep the chatter to a minimum. Only tell those you trust in the workplace, which if you are playing your cards right will be very few. A good way to squash the noise when asked is by saying something like this:

"I have been hired by company X and my last day here is (blank). I will miss working here very much, but I'm obligated to my new employer to not give any details of my new employment."

That should shut them up. All they want to know is if you got more money, and they don't need to know that anyway.

Watch out for short timers' syndrome as well. Short timers' syndrome will set in knowing you have no ties to where you are working and have another job waiting. Short timers' will cause you to get lazy and not really care about your job overall. Fight it off! You want to leave your company on good terms. Remember, you want the company you are leaving to regret letting you leave! Also with today's economy, you may have to come back for that old job if the new company lays you off or goes under. So it is best to leave on a high note.

Someone else leaving can be a good thing for your career, especially if that position coming vacant is a step up for you. Your company will have a process for filling the position and as soon as they know someone is leaving then the process will start. You should play a political chess move here. Whether you are going to apply for the new position or not, if it is within the scope of your job you should volunteer to do more. Go to the boss and let him know you have found out that Joe is leaving. Tell him that you realize that will leave the company short a man and you will be willing to pick up any extra slack in the meanwhile.

Don't ask for more money. Don't ask for a raise. Don't ask for your job description to be changed. Worry about all of that later. Put forth some effort first, worry about that.

This will give you a leg up when it is time for HR or your boss to start talking to folks about the empty slot. Companies love to promote from within. If you are already doing the job to cover for the person you are short, then you would be the natural choice. This also makes you look real good with the boss. Even if you have no intention of applying for the position, you should volunteer to do a little more while you are short handed. Your extra effort will score big points with the decision makers above you.

CHAPTER 15 QUICKIES:

- If you may be leaving, don't start slacking.
- Give as much notice as possible to your current employer, but only after you have signed on with the new company.
- Don't tell nosey co-workers anything.
- Be a professional and finish out your notice.

PART 3

MOVING UP

YOU ARE GETTING GOOD AT what you do! In fact, you are getting real good! The right people are starting to notice and you are ready to kick being a professional into high gear. That takes another level of commitment and if you have come this far, you don't have much farther to go. You need just a few more notches to get yourself over the top, so keep going!

This last section holds the information to help you position yourself for upward advance. Some of the chapters in this section may seem a bit trivial, even simple. That is the point my friend! What it takes to get that last look from your superiors in order to move you in to the next slot are the very things your co workers haven't caught on to. That extra effort in the right place, at the right time, makes all the difference.

Extra effort is the key phrase here. This is where you will start to color outside the lines, but in a good way. If you sit around and wait to get what you think you deserve, you will miss the boat. You have followed the recommendations in the previous sections to secure your place in the company, a solid accomplishment. However, a secure place is not where you what to be. Where you want to be is that next rung up the ladder. As soon as you stop trying to climb upward you have to worry about someone crawling over you to get to the next rung. So let's not get comfortable.

Promote, move up, and advance. All of those describe what you are trying to do and all of those words indicate something in common: action. They indicate motion in a direction and you can't move forward if you are sitting still waiting for something to happen. It's time to get aggressive!

CHAPTER 16

WHOSE JOB IS IT?

T HERE ARE TONS OF LITTLE things that go on in your company behind the scenes that someone does and is technically not their job. It's the little things that get done which make a difference. Those menial tasks are some of the things that don't actually fall in someone's job description. No one really knows when asked whose job it really is, it just gets done. In workplaces all across the world who actually does those little tasks remain a mystery.

Well from now on, it's your job. If no one owns it then you own it.

I am talking about everything that slips under the radar. Things like making the first pot of coffee in the morning. This could also be turning the coffee pot off and cleaning it out in the afternoon so it is ready for the next day. This is especially true if you help drink the coffee! I have personally witnessed a former boss of mine get more and more livid by the day at an employee who never helped clean the coffee pot! That sounds totally crazy, but the guy who never helped clean the pot or make coffee seemed to be in the first round of firings when it was that time. Kind of peculiar, huh?

Are you that girl or guy who seems to be the one that can fix the copier each time it jams up? If so, lend a hand whenever it goes down. Being relied on, even if in the beginning it is for the copier, gives you a stereotype. That positive stereotype is that you can be relied on when needed! Being reliable will grow to much more than the realm of the copier, I promise. Leaders want someone they can depend on.

Help welcome the new person to the office by volunteering to show them around. Give the guy a jump when his battery is dead because he left his lights on. Take your own trash out if the custodian is gone on vacation. You may even try being polite to the unpopular office nerd who is having a hard time of it at work.

I can hear your brain going off right now, "What the world did he just say??"

Yes guys and girls, you should be polite to them. You don't have to be best friends, but be polite. The reason for doing that is professionals realize their world is political. You never know, that person might be related to someone who could be high up in the company. I understand that the office dork may not be your favorite person, but they may be the favorite person of someone in a leadership position in the company. You may need that nerd someday on a technical project or to fix something technical you broke! In the professional world, who you know is just as important as what you know.

"Why should I do any of that behind-the-scenes junk? I will get taken advantage of!" You may be right, and sometimes you could get taken advantage of. But doing things that you think no one ever sees will help accomplish two different things.

One: It gets you noticed. You may not think it, and it may not happen every time, but it does happen. People will notice that you are helpful around the office or in the workplace. The people you work with will like it and your boss will like it. It keeps you on people's good side. You must play politics and stay on the good side of most folks because you never know when that person who is you co-worker will end up being your boss, or vice-versa.

Two: It builds character. Do something that will not directly benefit you once and a while. Do more than is expected of you. Exceed someone's expectations. It will help build your character and good character will be needed your entire life. Having a good, solid character is a quality shown by leaders. More importantly having good character is a quality of those promoted into leadership positions. You want that to be you!

Put forth that extra effort in any way you can. Don't go over the top and turn into a butt kisser, and don't be the guy who jumps up and down screaming "I helped do that! I helped do that!" You'll be marked as the company brown-noser and that's not the place you want to be either.

The older generations used to put it something like this: Be seen and not heard. That should be you. Be the helpful, silent type. Help clean up that spill when it happens. Take out your own trash. Clean up after yourself and even clean up after someone who left the mess once and a while.

Here is a good one. Let's say Monday morning you are the early one there—which is outstanding by the way. Once in a while stop and pick up a box of donuts. A couple dozen glazed will go a long way. Make the Monday morning pot and tell a few random people you brought extra donuts and to help yourself to one. No need to tell everyone your brought them, word will spread and people will know you put out a good gesture. It shows you were thinking about the team, not just yourself. Just make sure to clean up the mess from the boxes, I guarantee they will still be there long after the donuts are gone.

CHAPTER 16 QUICKIES:

- If no one owns it, you own it.
- Do something nice around the office.
- Build your character by doing things and expecting noting in return.
- Buy donuts once in awhile.
- Take charge of the office coffee pot.

Chapter 17

Drinking the Kool-Aide

WARNING: This chapter may leave a sour taste in your mouth. This is where you find out that you will have to kiss some butt every now and again. You will have to prop up someone's ego that generally may not know what the hell they are doing. Following your leader blindly into what looks to be disaster rings of drinking poisoned kool-aide. Granted, your corporate kool-aide will not be poisoned, but it certainly may taste like dirt. Aptly, that is the why I titled this chapter as such—because we all have to drink it from time to time.

Leaders in your organization will fall mostly into two categories. The first types are the ones who earned their stripes and know their stuff. We will call them the Type One Leader. They know not only their job but the company itself inside and out. They have been in the corporate trenches and have the battle scars to prove it. They are the rarest of leaders and are an invaluable asset. Most of you will be able to spot such leaders. If not, you will defiantly know who they are when they leave the company because half the company follows them out the door.

People who are not natural born leaders want to work for someone who is a type one leader. They want to know that someone sees all angles and has the company bases covered. That way they don't have to worry about anything but showing up and doing their job.

You will rarely have to worry about drinking any kool-aide from them. When they ask you to support a company initiative or project it's because they support it first and it is good for the company. When they ask you to do something it's because they know it is right or they did it before you. Granted, these types of leaders usually know when something has come down from corporate and is kool-aide. But these leaders can fix it and make it work. If you are fortunate enough to work for one of these leaders, learn all you can from them.

The second type of leader is somewhat more abundant. We will call them the Type Two Leaders. They are lacking much more in leadership skills and they may not have the pulse of what is going on in the company. They know how to make the kool-aide in 21 different flavors! I will say this; most of them did not start out that way. These types of leaders manage in a very hands-off style so that they are never directly responsible for any one thing. They let the lower level folks get in there and get dirty. That way if something goes wrong it will not be the fault of the higher up. They will be able to claim they had given the responsibility to their subordinate, thus absolving them of all wrong doing. I call this "Corporate Deferring" and it is pretty common place. Its sole purpose is that of self preservation. After all, when you are making mid 6 figures you will do everything possible to keep your job, right?

The company kool-aide will generally come from these type two leaders. They will spin it out in a variety of flavors and you will have to drink it. They won't ask you to fall on your sword, but you may have to get things done and go through considerable pains in doing so. The pain is in that you will have to work around their objectives because no actual thought or expectations have been put into what they want to do. Additional kool-aide drinking comes along when they ask how things are going. You must refrain from going into a 5 minute rant on how screwed up things are. Instead, you spin off your own form of kool-aide and say something like:

"There have been some opportunities but the team is making good progress. We will most certainly reach our goal!" They will pat you on the back and tell you what a great job you are doing then move on to the next shiny object they are chasing.

After that you may have to wash out your mouth from the sour taste and go get some help from the type one leader who will have some answers. The reason you do this is that there is no sense in ranting to the type two leader, they won't have any answers anyway.

There will also be corporate programs, projects or initiatives that are a total sham. You can see right through them and so can most everyone else. Destined for certain failure, type two leaders shamelessly promote the initiative. This is usually because it was their idea or they have something to gain from it first, company gain is then second. This agenda based leadership style is easy to spot because the good that may be derived from something is only seen from their point of view. The type two leaders don't always see the bigger picture or they are flat ignoring it.

What you must do is drink the kool-aide. Support the program or initiative quietly and publicly. Criticize it in private and only to those with whom you have great trust. If you are a true professional for change in your organization, you will try to right the wrong direction in order to avoid failure. Making the lemonade out of company lemons is tough work but in the end it will reward you. You start to become the guy or girl who can get things done. That is an admirable characteristic of a true professional and should be one of your goals.

Supporting something publicly and quietly means knowing when to shut up. This is a skill honed over time with lots of practice and learning from your mistakes. What makes it tough is that it is a two way street. There are times when you should not shut up and should speak up. When presented with this opportunity proceed with caution. Be positive and remain aware of the political game that has to be played from time to time. Saying the right thing at the right time is a balancing act. You don't want to be perceived as being negative all the time, it will get you left out of things.

Supporting lost causes, drinking the kool-aide, kissing butt, saying the right things at the right times and knowing when to shut up are all examples of corporate politics. You will find volumes information on the subject out there. Read up from time to time as you career progresses, it can only help. There will also be those type one leaders that will share the knowledge of navigating the corporate political world with you. If you feel that this person wouldn't knowingly steer you in the wrong direction, listen to every word. Their wisdom is money in the bank and can save you from some hard learned mistakes if you will humble yourself and apply their shared knowledge. I highly advise you to do so.

CHAPTER 17 QUICKIES:

- Find the type 1 leader in your organization and follow them.
- Find the type 2 leaders in your organization to be aware of where the kool-aide will come from.
- Become the "go to" guy or girl in you organization for getting things done.

Chapter 18

Off Time Invites

SOME OF YOU ARE LUCKY enough to have some skill or hobby that will come of good use to you in your career. You may be a natural on the golf course or perhaps you have great fashion sense. Or you may just have more free time than anyone else and you can put that to work on your off time, which serves a very specific purpose for your career.

All you natural born golfers will probably be in high demand for your company golf tournament. Your end game could also benefit the Executive leaders of the company with their own golf game. When asked, always be truthful about what you shoot. Don't talk your game up like you can shoot a 70 when you don't know the difference between a wood and an iron. Your little lie will be discovered quickly and then you will never be asked again.

If you get asked, by all means go. Make time even if it is on your only day off. Show up early and shoot your best. And if your partner happens to be your boss then carry his game if you have to. If you can make good on how you say you play then your name will travel in the small circles at the top as the guy they want on their team and that is a great thing.

Don't wait around to be asked. If your company has charity golf tournaments then sign up to play. If there is no company tournament or it has already passed, put golf memorabilia on your desk. When the COO walks by and sees a golf ball with a date on it he will defiantly ask what that was for.

"Oh that was when I shot my best game of a 69 last year."

"Really?! We should talk golf, maybe go out and hit a few" will surely be his reply. He is not worried about his ego because he out ranks you. By having you as a golf partner it is good for his image because you help his team win. This is good for you, even if it is his team.

Perhaps you are one of those young women who know how to dress professionally but still keep a great fashion sense. You will get picked out by your female boss for your taste and style. She'll want to know where you got it and if it was on sale. She'll want to know "your secret." By all means tell her your secret! Before long she may want you to do something on a Saturday like go to the mall to help her pick out better clothes. Now someone of your age may not look forward to hanging out with someone who is 25 years your senior and helping them shop. Do it anyway and do it gladly.

You should take note when she comes in wearing something new and if you have that type of working relationship, tell her how great it looks and ask her the same "where'd you get it!?" questions she asks you.

Guys, this is a girls club so don't even try it.

Some of you may not be fortunate to have a golf game or a fashion sense (like me). If that is the case then you need to be volunteering at the charity events your company hosts. Blood drives, be there. Road side clean ups, volunteer! Toys for tots, sign up. Anything that your company will put its own name on then you better sign up as close to the top as you can get.

All of this has one distinct purpose that I spoke of earlier. It might not get you a raise or a promotion—but they remember your charity or kindness when doing your review. They will remember you shot a 68 in the last tournament and help win. They remember the shopping trip you took with them. It is not supposed to influence someone but we are human and we are easily influenced sometimes. That helps and is a plus, but it is not the bottom line. The objective is to get your name out there in a positive way so that leadership knows you exist.

Another way for you to do this is to find a company publication with all of your leaders pictures and bio's on them. Learn their faces and their names. That is so when you walk past them in the hall instead of just nodding like an idiot you can say "Good morning Mr. Leader, how are you?" Fates and fortunes are started in a passing hallway conversation, trust me.

I once walked into a company bathroom followed by another man I didn't see at first and I didn't pay any attention to who he was. After handling my business I went to wash my hands (you better always do that, someone could be taking note of you not washing your hands). When I finally saw his faced I realized who he was, which happened to be one of the Executive leaders of the company.

He looked over and said: "I better wash my hands real good around you, I have heard about your food safety classes and I don't want to get on your bad side!" he said jokingly. It was just his way of being pleasant and a bit funny. What stood out to me was he had never been in any class I taught and I have never discussed food safety with him, but he knew who I was. That's the point.

Now guys, if you know he is one of the bosses don't speak unless spoken to. If he is one of those men not comfortable talking to you with his Johnson in his hand, he will be *real* uncomfortable if you try and strike up a conversation!

Like it or not your boss and the leadership of the company make the promotion decisions. You will never get promoted by default. If they don't know who the heck you even are then you can't get ahead in the promotion line. So get your name out there!

CHAPTER 18 QUICKIES:

- Accept off time invites if they are appropriate.
- Volunteer at company functions.
- Try you best to get you name out there.
- Learn the names and faces of company leadership so you can strike up a friendly conversation.

Chapter 19

MEETINGS

MEETINGS IN THE WORK PLACE are important. They are a pinnacle of importance to some, could be for most. Going to meetings is like getting out and heading to that trendy club. There is something going on in the company and you have been invited! Think of them that way and not as a burden.

Since meetings are where you want to be, the first rule of meetings is always go. If your company uses a calendar tool to manage all this, such as Microsoft, as soon as you receive an email invite accept it immediately. Don't be that person that leaves the meeting in your inbox until the last minute then decide whether or not to go. Don't double and triple book your meetings as a "maybe" then pick one at the last minute. If the person has requested you to be there it is for a reason. If you have a previous meeting, tell them that or suggest a new time.

It may be possible that you don't know the person inviting you or you have no clue what the meeting is about. Don't ask; you don't care, just go. Someone thinks enough of you to have invited you because you hopefully will bring something to the table. You do not want to be seen wandering around the office asking people annoying questions like:

"Who is this person? Do you know what this is about? Are you going to this meeting? I don't understand what we are meeting about??"

Again, don't ask—you don't care, just go.

That annoying person asking all those questions about "why this?" and "who is that?" is the most likely person to not get invited to the next big meeting. You are too much of a pain in the butt to be even worth inviting. The person holding the meeting or heading up the "who should be there" list for her boss is the person you annoyed the crap out of asking all those questions. Again, don't ask—you don't care, just go.

Show up early for the meeting and be prepared. Start keeping a notebook to take meeting notes in so they don't get lost or misplaced. Be sure and write down what the meeting is about along with the date and time. Also note everyone in attendance. Some of the notes will be a formality and just stay filed away. There are quite a few occasions when you will need to call on those notes to review some details. It will really add to your professional image when your boss asks if you remember something from that meeting last week and you pull out your notes for a quick response. That shows you were paying attention and reminds your boss why he hired you.

Unless you are on a webinar or video conference and need you laptop, leave it in your office. The person who is hosting the meeting will be completely irritated if you bring your computer so you can catch up on emails of finish typing a report. If you are that damn busy then don't bother coming. Meetings are not the time for emails and other work and it is unprofessional to do so! If you are a tech guy on a technical project then you are excused. If you are not then bringing your computer doesn't make you look any smarter or more important than you actually are.

During the meeting it may come about that there is a need to form a separate committee to research an issue or topic from the meeting. Or perhaps some leg work needs to be done by someone before the next meeting and the boss asks for some help. You should jump at the chance! Professionalism is always seen in those who go above and beyond and this is a great time to do that. If you get assigned a task in the meeting or are asked to provide someone in your office additional information discussed in the meeting, do so immediately. Odds are if you don't take care of it quickly you will get busy on something else and forget. It would be very unprofessional of you to do so and bad for your reputation!

Some of your meetings may have to take place in the early morning or late in the evening so that everyone may attend. There is nothing really to be done about these kinds of meetings and they are generally the exception, not the rule. Once in a great while you will be asked to come to a meeting that is very important, but falls on your off time. There will be nothing you can do about it, so just suck it up and get it over with. However, treat that day just as any other work day. Don't show up in your soft ball uniform on your way to a game; remain professional!

Meetings are a part of business culture you will get used to. Professionals treat them as opportunities to advance or prove their worth to the company. Approach meetings with this professional attitude and accept the challenges that come with them.

CHAPTER 19 QUICKIES:

- If possible go to all the meetings you are invited to.
- Keep meeting notes in a notebook.
- Leave your laptop at your desk.
- Volunteer for additional tasks that may come from the meeting.

Chapter 20

Special Assignments

ONE EARLY MORNING YOUR BOSS will call on you. He will ask you to come to his office and close the door. The thoughts will race through your head trying to figure out what you did wrong and why he is getting ready to fire you!! "Man I really thought I was doing a great job!" you will be screaming silently. Fear not my professional friend; this is a good closed door session. You boss has something special he needs you to work on. This special assignment could be a number of things such as a special project, special account or picking up a task that someone else was working on which they wrecked.

You accept the challenge immediately in case you were wondering.

Don't go asking about special compensation or if you'll make more or get a special bonus. You will be missing the point if that is where you go with this. You will also be marked as a haggler and out for yourself, not what you can do to further the company. You boss has called on you because you are a professional. You can handle more than the rest of your co-workers so he thinks he can expect more. It is you job to exceed his expectations.

Sitting in your boss' office there are some things you should do here. I know you brought you meeting note book and are taking notes, aren't you? Good! Make sure to write down everything he is saying. Know what his expectations are. You may have a leader type that has not asked what the goal is for this special assignment. If you are sure it has not been stated or is unclear to you, by all means ask. That might go something like:

"Sir, just so I understand; what is the overall objective or expectation you want to see when this is accomplished?"

That will be perceived as being forward thinking and results oriented. That is a good thing for your boss to think about you!

Your boss will normally give you a time frame for this assignment as well. If he or she does not, ask that too. You need to know when they expect it done—exactly. There is a big difference between today and tomorrow when it comes to deadlines if you forget to ask. When you have the deadline, consider that set in stone. Your goal when it comes to that deadline is to meet or exceed the expected timeframe. Meet or beat it at all costs! Work nights or weekends till you get it wrapped up. Do not procrastinate!

Some of the special assignments may be more team oriented. This may be a group project or research you have been chosen to be a part of. This is just as important and you should take it seriously. If you get to pick the team, get the best people you can find. If you need help finding people who will help your team succeed ask the type one leaders in your organization to help you select team members.

In the team setting, you should always be a part of the solution, not part of the problem. Negativity and naysayers will quickly be cast out. Be positive, supportive and proactive in what the group is doing. Contribute to the discussions or research as much as you possibly can. When group or team meetings are scheduled, you should make time to attend every one. The project leader, if it is not you, will have to report on the groups' progress. If a particular area of the project is behind or lacking and it is discovered that you never attend any team meetings, you will be in a bad spot. Professionals show up and contribute to the efforts.

Professionals also get things done. A goal in your professional journey should be to get things done and not just what is part of your job description. Special projects, assignments and tasks are assigned by leaders within your organization. Leaders do not like to fail. If you fail it is a direct reflection on them and their ability to choose professionals within the organization. Take these assignments very seriously.

CHAPTER 20 QUICKIES:

- Accept all special assignments and execute them to the best of your ability.
- Make sure to get a time frame and expectations for your assignment.
- If on a team assignment, become a valuable part of the team.

Chapter 21

Performance Reviews

Performance reviews will play a major role in getting a promotion. At minimum you will have to have a satisfactory rating on your last review to get a promotion. You will defiantly have to have that rating for any kind of raise.

Basically, your performance review is a report card. This tool is so that your employer can tell you how they think you are doing at your job. You get a rating, which is usually on a numeric scale or descriptive terms. That rating determines your eligibility to get promoted or get a raise. Your professional goal should be to have a good review each and every time you get one. This track record will follow you for your entire term at the company. Bad reviews may leave you in a bad light for future leaders who manager you. It is always best for your tenure at your employer to not have any baggage from poor reviews hanging around.

Most people will get taken by surprise by their performance review. Not at the results but what they are graded on. Every company uses their own method of review and every company is different. They may grade on anything and everything. The key to not being surprised is to know up front what you will be graded on. After your 90 days has past, ask your supervisor or Human Resource manager for a copy of the review form or policy. This will be a good eye opener for you and let you know what you should be on the lookout for. Knowing this information up front is also a sign of a true professional.

The timing for a review is also different from one company to the next. Some will do a review after 90 days or 6 months in your current position. Most will just do one every year. At review time, be proactive. Come to your review with a list of business goals you have made for yourself to work towards over the next year. Listen intently at what your reviewer has to say. If your review is done properly it will only contain the facts. Do yourself a favor and don't try and argue the facts or justify them. If they tell you that you are rated 'unsatisfactory' in attendance because you missed 5 days last year, that's on you. You will likely discuss the topic and get to make written comments. Always be positive. State that you plan on doing better in your performance and how you will work proactively on this issue. Do not react negatively about the subject, it will only make things worse and it is very unprofessional. A true professional will accept valid criticism for their lack of performance and make it a point to do better. Valid criticism is a useful tool to a professional because it lets them know what others think they should work on, not just what they see or don't see.

Raises are a sensitive subject when it comes to a review. Most companies will not allow a boss to make up a raise amount that you get. Your rating will equal to a number and those numbers will usually translate to a percent raise in your salary. So even if your boss thinks you are great, it will be out of their hands to give you a bigger raise.

In today's economy, raises are usually small. Don't be shocked if you get a good rating on your review but only get 1% or 2% for a raise. Your company may actually freeze raises as well. Remember in the first chapter where I said you make your deal going in the door? This is why I said that. Raises are tough to come by and if you think you will be able to dramatically increase your income by relying on your raises you are sorely mistaken.

If the 2% raise happens to you (and it will, I promise), don't get angry or offended. There is nothing that arguing with your reviewer will accomplish. Usually what will happen is they give you a good review but tell you unfortunately they are only allowed to give you 2% and that has applied to everyone in the company. State you are disappointed about the amount but understand why. That is about as far as you can go. It is also being professional because you have stated how you feel about the situation without being negative. Saying nothing or being negative will leave you feeling like you have been taken advantage of. Going that route will lead you towards resenting the company you work for. Then you start slacking in your performance, your professionalism suffers and you are on your way out the door—either by your own doing or the companies' decision. To avoid all that, say your peace and move on.

The whole review process may be a very big deal at your company, or it may just be another thing they spin the company kool-aide over. If so, don't take much stock in it. Find out what information you can from those you trust in your workplace about how reviews go. If it appears to be a lackadaisical event just do what you can to keep your rating high, but don't focus on making more money because of them. Set your sights on working towards that next promotion and earn your money that way.

CHAPTER 21 QUICKIES:

- Know about your company's performance reviews.
- Have a list of business goals for yourself when you go in for your review.
- You will never get ahead relying on raises to earn more money.
- Don't get worked up if the review process is a joke, worry about a promotion!

Chapter 22

Professional Colleagues

FROM THE TIME YOU START your journey as a professional you will begin to build professional business relationships in many different directions. Some will be colleagues you respect and admire in your own company. Some will be colleagues from other companies you have grown to know and respect in your dealings with one another. Vendors will also be a part of professional relationships that are built as you get to know them when they provide services or goods to your company. Everywhere you look you will start to see other professional minded people like yourself. Some of them you will get to know better and start to build a professional history with.

These relationships are invaluable. There are so many useful aspects for putting time and energy into these it will be hard for me to sum up. Some will be worth more of your time than others. You will form your own opinion of how to gauge this throughout your career.

It pays to know what is going on in the business world. Other professionals in your industry are great sources of networking. They can share pain they are working through in their company and solutions they have come across. They can be inside sources for personnel and employees you may or may not want to hire. They will generally share, on a limited basis, what is going on in their company or what they hear about other companies. You of course, will do the same as this is a mutual benefit to you both. Your discussions with other colleagues on industry trends will look good for you when your boss brings up the subject in the next department meeting. Keep it somewhat mysterious as to not reveal your sources. Colleagues deserve discretion for their faith they have bestowed in you and they should return the favor. Your boss will think you a smart and savvy professional with his or her finger on the pulse of your industry. That is the position you want to be in!

Another great benefit is you never know where your next job will come from. How many people have you come across that got their job somewhere because they knew someone that worked at the company they were applying for? Again, it is not always what you know but who you know. If that former colleague is a professional acquaintance of yours and you need to apply with his company, you will end up having a great reference. Human Resources will show slight favor to those applying for a job when someone from within the company gives a good reference. Even when dealing with other companies and you happen to be competing for business, remain professional. Competing in a fair and legitimate manner instead of cutting people's throats will be remembered. Be tough, but always remain courteous, honest and respectful. It will take you a lot farther.

The business world is very vast and large but it runs in small circles. At many points in my career I have come across a person I had worked with 5 or 10 years ago. That professional history can pay off for both you and your colleague. Try not to burn too many professional bridges with the people you work for or work with.

You will want to be careful when it comes to vendor relationships. Some vendors will throw all kinds of freebies or swag your way to try and influence you. Your company may have strict policies against this, but vendors may try anyway to get some perceived advantage with you. If you company finds out you took those tickets to the game from them, you are destined to get the axe. If the rules are vague as to the subject of vendor gifts, ask your boss or Human Resources first. It is better to be safe than sorry with this subject.

Make sure you keep your professional contacts backed up in some form, preferable at a location you can get to. If your computer crashes and you lose you contact file, all will be lost—so have a backup. If you get fired and are told to clear your desk out with a security guard standing there, you won't have time or be able to. Always keep the professional colleagues you want to stay in touch with throughout your career in a personal file.

CHAPTER 22 QUICKIES:

- Other professionals are a great source of networking in your industry.
- You may be able to utilize a professional colleague for a reference or job lead in the future.
- Keep your professional contacts backed up and have a personal copy.

CHAPTER 23

INTEGRITY IN THE WORKPLACE

U NLESS YOU HAVE BEEN LIVING under a rock, you are aware of what has been going on in and around Wall Street lately. Corporate greed destroying companies, CEO's putting themselves before the entire company and hundreds of millions of dollars in salaries and bonuses to those that do not deserve it. In the end it was each the company shareholders that paid, along with us taxpayers. It was almost like the place got robbed and we watched the guy do it and knew who he was. It's hard to forget someone that robs and steals who doesn't wear a mask and never uses a gun! The corporate crooks have given professionals a bad name. The crooks all have different stories, but they have one singular thing in common. Across the board, no matter what the industry was, somewhere along the way each one of those people lost their professional integrity. Lost is probably the wrong word, it is more like threw it away.

Professionalism in the workplace is a quality that fewer and fewer people have. Integrity in the workplace is another trait that is circling the drain very fast. You as the next generation of professionals will be charged with reviving the era of integrity. There are a lot of things that make up integrity, most of which is pride. I do not mean being cocky. I'm talking about pride in what you do and the company you work for. I am talking about the positive kind of pride. You should be proud that you work for a company that offers the best product, service or support for their perspective industry. You should have pride in what you do! Pat yourself on the back once and a while for a job well done! Take pride in the professional people that work for you and the job they do every day. Praise their efforts and give them the recognition they deserve! Pride and professionalism go hand in hand. They are both positive characteristics that complement one another. Having both qualities will contribute to your success in a great way!

Another trait that goes along with having integrity is quality. Some companies make that their number one focus. Ever heard a company say that quality is the #1 priority? You may hear a lot of companies use that in more than one area of their business. They may be talking about a quality product, quality employees or quality service. In one form or another, the word quality will be a part of your workplace as well. In whatever form your company promotes quality, you should support that same effort 110%! Strive for the best quality you can provide your customer or company every time the opportunity presents itself. Don't settle for "OK"—not ever. If you have employees working under you, don't let them settle for "OK" either. Professionals put forth their best and expect the best. You should put forth your best effort in everything you do. Don't do anything halfway, go above and beyond the expectation every chance you get. If you make that your motto it will be a win-win, both for you and your company.

Professionals end up having to make decisions. More times than not they have to make lots of decisions and make them dozens of times a day. Some of them will be easy, some of them tough. In everything you do as a professional you should do the right thing each time. Integrity means you do the right thing no matter what. Professionals with integrity will do the right thing when nobody is looking. They do the right thing and expect nothing in return. Do what is right for your customer, for your employee and for your company. Ever hear the old saying of always telling the truth because it's easier to remember? The truth may be a difficult thing to hear or say sometimes, but it is the right thing. Did you make a mistake? Admit it and correct it. That is the right thing to do. If a customer gets a bad product from your company, apologize and make it right by replacing it or refunding their money. That is the right thing to do. Now sometimes you may be given a choice between the right thing and taking the easy way out. However the easy way is a lie. When that situation presents itself I implore you to do the right thing. I promise you will be better off in the end. Knowingly doing the wrong thing will have its way of coming back around to you. Remain a steadfast professional and do the right thing!

A final thought on integrity is how to go about it. Putting all of that together means pride, quality, putting forth your best effort and doing the right thing. There are too many things to remember how to do if you don't conduct yourself consistently. Therefore, in all of your dealings you want to remain professional and you should conduct yourself in the same manner each time. You have just learned what to do. Here is how to go about doing it. Do it always with courtesy, honesty and respect. Deal with your boss, your employees, fellow co-workers and your customers all in the same manner. Treat each person with courtesy, honesty and respect. Using those words as a guideline in all of your dealings will be the pillar of your success. Keep those three things in mind and you won't go wrong. The way of courtesy, honesty, and respect is the choice of the true professional!

CHAPTER 23 QUICKIES:

- Take pride in what you do and where you work.
- Strive for the best quality you possibly can.
- Do the right thing—always.
- Always use courtesy, honesty, respect.

AFTERWORD

YOU CONTROL YOU OWN FATE. The level of your success that you can achieve is only limited by you. If you are one of the few that has decided to be more, then I applaud you! You are today's generation and you are a professional! That is something truly amazing to accomplish! You will continue throughout your professional journey and will do many other things by taking control of your own fate. Never let your fate be dictated to you.

When you cut your potential off to be something in life by using your childhood, education or knowledge base as your excuse then you are selling yourself short. I realize that things happen which are out of your control. How you respond to those things that happen will be where you end up taking control of your own fate. You control your own fate moving forward, no one else.

If you don't have the knowledge base or education then go out and get it. You can learn anything! It will take commitment and dedication but if you have come this far then you already posses those traits. However it will take one other thing which most people seem to miss. It will take an expectation.

That expectation is what you want of yourself. You cannot just go; you have to know where you are going and what you want. If you still are not able to come up with that then at least decide you don't want to be where you are *now*. At least do that much and then it will be easier to lay down your own path of your own choosing.

If I said I had $1000 in my pocket and you could ask for as little or as much as you wanted, what would you ask for? Would you say "Just give me whatever you want?" Not a chance! You would go right for the jugular and ask for the whole thousand dollars, right? Of course you would!

That needs to be the same mentality that you approach your whole life with. Decide what you want—then go out and get it. Don't wait for it to fall in your lap, go and get it. Fight tooth and nail for what you want if you have to. You must go out and stake your own claim to what you want out there in the world, especially in the business world.

In today's world, time is the most precious commodity. I thank you for deciding to put forth the time from your own life to read through this book. I hope that you have learned something. I hope that you have taken away more from this book than expected. I hope your vision of what it takes to be professional is a bit clearer now. I hope your success exceeds your expectations.

You are the future of whatever you have chosen to be a professional in. You should believe that about yourself because if you truly have read this book, then I believe that about you.